Thanksgiving

The **power** to **transform** your life

A daily devotional to bring you into the presence of God

Stella Doggett

Published by
The Centre for Life Management
172 Long Street,
Dordon, England.
B78 1QA
www.lifetraining.co.uk,

ISBN 978-1-7392333-0-3

Cover design by Sian James @cre8sian_art@yahoo.com
Typeset by Angela Selfe
Project managed by theweddedhare@gmail.com

Acknowledgements

I would like to thank all those who have helped to bring this project together. The many friends who have encouraged me along the way, especially the lovely Jean who has cooked and kept the show on the road here in Dordon, releasing me to type and edit my work, and my dear Canadian friend Dena who has believed in me and encouraged me for over 50 years. And most importantly my husband Mark, my 'joint heir of the grace of life', (1 Peter 3:7, AMP.) who has been my soul mate and partner now for 43 years; our lifetime together of adventuring with the Lord. He has now faithfully and patiently encouraged me, contributed to, edited, and checked the biblical references for these daily readings. Without your company on our journey of life with Jesus, these readings would have been far less rich and may never have seen the light of day.

Introduction

Having posted several blogs during the 2020 Covid 'Lockdowns', I asked the Lord what He was wanting to say to His people going into 2021. I was surprised and excited to hear Him say that He wanted to release a spirit of gratitude over His people. He wanted to shift the mindset of His followers to embrace gratitude as a lifestyle.

This I believe was, and is, to position us to live above the chaos of the world at this time, and to instead be 'light' in the darkness. It is also about preparing our hearts for revival. Now is 'our turn to shine' Isaiah 60:1,2.

It seemed that the Lord was saying to me that if I would write it down, He would give me a message on 'Thanksgiving' each day for the next 365 days. And He did! I initially delivered these as a daily blog and now, encouraged by friends, I am publishing them as this daily devotional book.

This is not about 365 things for which we can be thankful, because there are many, many more than 365 of those. This is about the power of thanksgiving in our lives and the transformation it works in us and for us, as it brings us into God's presence.

This book that you now have in your hand contains the first three months of those devotionals for you to read and to enjoy: days 1 - 91. The days are not dated because some will read it daily, whilst for others one meditation may last longer, perhaps a few days. Some have used the scriptures and thoughts of one day as a basis for their home group meetings, and some as inspiration for a talk or a word of encouragement for others.

On each day you will find a suggested activation. Personalising these suggestions will help you to be a 'doer' of the word and not just a 'hearer', (James 1:23). On some days you will find spaces in which you can write, or draw, your own thoughts, meditations or prayers.

Sometimes the scriptures to which I have referred are written out, at other times there is just a biblical reference. I would encourage having a Bible at your side so that you can read these passages for yourself.

Please use these reflections in your own way, and let the Holy Spirit bless you and fill you as you 'Enter His Gates' and find Him to be all that you need. I pray that this journey of 365 days will increasingly transform your relationship with the Almighty, and hence your life!

DAY 1 | of our journey to live thankfully – 'fully giving our thanks to our God'

Our journey into a life of thanksgiving must start with Psalm 100. In this Psalm we are encouraged to shout, sing and serve the Lord with gladness, because He is good, He made us and we are His 'flock.' Then in verse 4 we see that in **thanksgiving** we have a wonderful key that will open the gate into God's presence, enabling us to enter right into His courts. We read ...

'Enter His gates with thanksgiving and His courts with praise;
give thanks to Him and praise His name.
For the Lord is good and His love endures forever;
His faithfulness continues through all generations.'

Our thanksgiving and praise actually bring us into His courts. Why? Because there is only praise and thanks for Jesus in heaven; no doubts, no fears, and no unbelief can exist there. Thanksgiving and gratitude and praise fill the heavenly realm and so our thanksgiving aligns us with heaven's atmosphere, facilitating our access to the throne of God. It also, I believe, catches His EAR and draws us close to His HEART.

Thanksgiving is the way in which, when we come to our Heavenly Father, we can very quickly connect with Him. We may have lots to ask Him, things to tell Him, or even 'pour out to Him' in lament, Psalm 62:8, but our thanksgiving is a big key to enabling the face to face audience that we want with Him.

Melissa Helser, singing spontaneously in 2022 before a worship recording time sang ... *'We've got ten thousand 'thank yous' to give you. We run through the gates, we approach the throne of grace. A thousand 'thank yous' pouring out our mouths. Ten thousand 'thank yous' like a water fall on your throne ...'* – a psalm for our day perhaps?

How delighted the Lord must be with that offering of thanks that we pour out on His throne, and how thrilled the Lord is with our gratitude. Why? Because it signals that we, His people, have 'grasped' something of His infinite goodness and of His 'love that surpasses mere knowledge.' Ephesians 3:19. AMP. So every day **and especially** when you feel a bit distant from God, or somewhat lost as to what He is saying to you, or where He is leading you, 'give thanks to Him.'

If your mind is blank and you don't know what to thank Him for, ask the Holy Spirit, our wonderful 'alongside helper' to refresh your mind and heart about the things for which you can thank Him. In this very biblical way you can open the gate for yourself, right into His presence, on a daily . Then, over the next days, weeks and months we are going to see how ksgiving' not only blesses God and brings us into His presence, but t also transforms us from the inside out.

Erratum:
Day 1, page 7, 'My prayer at the start of this journey'
The reference should be Hebrews 4:16

vation ...

would you like to grow in your personal, individual journey of ormation through thanksgiving in this coming year? Jot down any cal ways that might help you to go forward like a) having a specific ɔ reflect on the day's scriptures, or b) keeping a journal of 'truths' that rd highlights to you, or c) you might like to use the prayer below as ;in these days of discovering 'the power of thanksgiving'.

rayer at the start of this journey ...

God, my Abba, I thank you so much that you want me to live in your ;e at all times, and I thank you that I can enter into your presence as ɔu thanks.

Lord Jesus, thank you so much that you have made it possible for me to come to the Father. Thank you that because of your death on the cross I have full access to Him and can draw near with boldness. Hebrews 5:16.

Holy Spirit thank you that you are my 'alongside helper' at all times, and I ask you to especially be that helper and guide on this journey into the Father's heart and presence through thanksgiving. Amen

DAY 2 | Why we need to be thankFULL

The word 'Thankful', gives it away. Thank FULL. If you are FULL of thanks it is so honoring to God and it also stops you being filled by any other thoughts that the enemy would want to put into your mind. I mean all that negative stuff about yourself, your life, other people, or even God Himself.

ThankFULLness can also drive away those negatives that are already there. We can illustrate it in this way. If you want to get the air out of a glass, a vacuum pump might do it but the air will rush back in at the exact same moment that you remove the pump. A much simpler way to extract the air from a vessel is just to fill it with a liquid. It's called displacement.

As a young Christian, I was going through a difficult time, experiencing a lot of perplexity with the Lord over things that were happening (or not happening) in my life, and so I was not in a peaceful place with the Lord. During that time a very dear Christian friend, Dena, sent me a cassette to listen to (yes I'm that old!). It was a recording of some Christian songs. The words of the song through which the Lord spoke strongly to me that day are still etched on my memory, and they are:-

*'With my hands lifted up and my mouth **filled** with praise,*
***with a heart of thanksgiving** I will bless you always'.*

Listening to this song restored my peace because, I think, as I listened and allowed the Holy Spirit to fill my heart with thankfulness, that same thanksgiving drove out all the disagreements with God that I was harbouring; disagreements over the way life was going for me at that time. Being thankFULL (not just a gritted teeth job) keeps us in harmony with the Lord. It keeps us enjoying His friendship and it keeps us filled with His joy.

ThankFULLness is so different to just 'saying' thank you. We all know what it is like to give someone something, or to do something special for someone, and then to hear (spoken or unspoken) in response a "thank you ... but I'd rather have had ... a ... b ... or c ...!"

ThankFULLness is different to a formal 'Thank You', because it actually expresses my agreement with the heart of God for me, and with His working in my life. Now we all know the answer to the rhetorical question, 'Can two walk together unless they be agreed?' Amos 3: 3, and therefore we know that agreeing with God is a big key to staying in step with Him.

ThankFULLness leaves no room for the negative, the doubts and fears, the suspicions that God is not quite doing right by us and the disagreement with God's ways with us. We know that this is important because, left unchecked, those gripes can perhaps become 'The little foxes that spoil the vineyard.' Song of Songs 2:15.

It's important to note here that ThankFULLness is not about suppressing our doubts and fears but rather about making a way for us to talk with the Lord and to share with our loving Heavenly Father, those things which we don't understand.

And finally thankFULLness enables us to hear and receive His wisdom on these matters, or simply His peace if things still remain a mystery.

Activation . . .

Is there something in your life right now that you don't understand, or struggle with; an area of life where you would like to come into agreement with the Lord? Use the space below to bring that area to the Lord with thanksgiving in your heart for His goodness, His love and His plans for you, and ask Him for His peace and wisdom as you go forward.

DAY 3 | Thankfulness that helps the memory

In Psalm 103 we are exhorted to 'Bless the Lord' and to 'not forget all His benefits'. How extraordinary that we can have the privilege of 'blessing' the source of all blessing. What an incredible thought that our gratitude can bless God's heart – make Him happy!!! Amazing! The God of all joy and gladness can be 'blessed' by us, and it's such a simple thing to do. Giving thanks does not depend on age, education, income or being in the right place, rather it is something we can choose to do whenever we want and wherever we are.

I was recently greatly moved by realising that God is delighted when I am delighted by what He has done for me, or by what He has given me. Little children are so good at this. How many of us have not experienced the sheer joy and affection we feel for a little child when we have given them something that really delights them. It is so very different to when a gift is accepted but there is just a formal 'thank you' as the gift is put to one side.

Slowing down to thank Him, for the beauty around you, or for an item of food or clothing you love, for a friend, or for something in your home, sets a pattern of 'noticing' His loving care and goodness in the every day and ordinary. Asking the Holy Spirit to highlight God's goodness to us in our everyday life is so important. This is because we miss so much of His goodness to us in our haste, and in our preoccupation with all that needs to be done in our 'oh so busy' lives.

At school, at dinner time, we used to have to say 'grace'. It went, "For what we are about to receive may the Lord make us truly thankful." I'm not sure how much this 'blessed' God's heart. It is in fact more like a prayer addressing God in the third person, almost implying that we are not really thankful. I think He would probably rather hear, "Wow, Lord! Those chips look great! Thank you so much for potatoes, and for those who have turned them into chips, and those who have cooked them. I love you!"

As we grow into living a life *filled* with thanksgiving, we will become a people who take nothing for granted, who remember all the things, big and small, that He does for us daily. As a result we will find so much more connection with our wonderful heavenly Father as we sense His joy in our joy. We will also be taking more seriously the psalmist's exhortation in Psalm 103 to 'not forget all His benefits' as we set *our* hearts to bless **His heart**. What a privilege!

Activation…

Try and recall, and then write a list below, of some of the things that you have taken for granted from this last week. Things for which you would now like to thank God:-

Thank God that I'm Alive

Thank God for freash clothes Afte a semub In Tub

Thank God for people

All In the Image of God there beautiful me see Jesus In the Faces of little Children

Then ask the Holy Spirit to now give you a heart of gratitude and an ability to notice the richness of the Lord's provision and His blessings in your everyday life, especially for those things that you may have been taking for granted.

(My Home)

Safe neighbonhood

DAY 4 | Thanksgiving when we need a miracle!

We can naturally find it easy to thank God when He has blessed us in some special way, but what about thanking Him when we are faced with a great need. In Luke 9:12 -17, Jesus shows us how it's done! Have a look at the feeding of the 5,000 retold for us there. Jesus is faced with meeting a huge need for food with just five loaves and two fishes. So He took the loaves and fish, looked up to heaven, **gave thanks** and blessed them, and then got the disciples to distribute the food until all were fed – 'satisfied' we are told – and there was still a mountain of food left over.

I believe we need to see that 'thanksgiving often precedes the miracle'. When we look up to heaven and give thanks as Jesus did, we are not looking at **the demand, the need,** or **the supply,** but we are lifting our gaze to heaven. We are joining our heart with God's heart, and all the resources of heaven.

The miracle happened after Jesus had told them what He wanted them to do. "Give them something to eat." When we have a need, or we feel that the Lord is calling us to do something that is beyond our ability to do, or beyond our resources, let's first do what the disciples did: offer Him our meager resources, and then let's do what Jesus did: **Give thanks to our heavenly Father.**

Then, whether our desire is to be able to meet someone's need, or for wisdom in a situation, for strength to do something, for courage to act or speak, or to give beyond our means – whatever it might be – when we offer our contribution to God with thanksgiving, **we are joining our resources to His**. We are partnering with heaven and we will see the miracle as we go forward.

How it must delight God's heart, as we express our confidence in His wonderful presence with us by thanking Him. It also helps us to 'stay in faith' as we wait for the miracle. In Romans 4:18-21 we have a wonderful example of this. We read that Abraham 'grew strong in faith as He gave glory to God.' I think 'thanksgiving' must have been a big part of his 'growing strong' in faith as he awaited the miracle son he had been promised. I also think that his thanksgiving was a part of what gave God a lot of glory at this time.

It is important to note here that 'giving thanks' is not some way of manipulating God into doing what we want, but a way of expressing our trust in Him that He is with us. As we do that, we can then listen for direction in the situation, or receive the faith to wait.

Activation ...

Practice giving thanks "before the miracle" in the challenges of your everyday life, and grow strong in your faith for those bigger things that will come your way.

You can start very simply with a prayer like this.

'Dear Lord, I thank you that you are with me, that you know the situation here, that you love me and that you want to demonstrate your glory through this situation. Thank you that you multiplied loaves and fishes, and that you can multiply the meager resources that I have and that I am offering to you now in Jesus name.'

As you speak to the Lord with this kind of thanksgiving in your heart and on your lips, let faith rise up and then allow the Holy Spirit to lead you as to what to do or say next.

Have fun!

DAY 5 | Thanksgiving to appropriate God's promises

One amazing way in which we can increase our faith is by using thanksgiving to make scripture personal. Thanking God for the truths in His word draws us into a closer friendship with the Lord. Let's take for example the 23rd Psalm and put an 'I thank you' in front of each phrase. We can then read it slowly and specifically **to the Lord** as He sits alongside us in our room.

'I thank you Lord that you are my shepherd and that means I shall never be in want.

I thank you Lord that you lead me to green pastures where I can lie down, be at rest and nourished.

I thank you Lord that you lead me by still waters and refresh my soul.

I thank you Lord that you guide me in good and right paths, even for your own names' sake.

I thank you that you walk with me through the dark valleys of life where there is death, that you are with me to strengthen me and keep me going, so that I don't need to be afraid.

I thank you that even in the presence of my enemies (great difficulties) you prepare a feast and provide for me.

I thank you that you anoint my head with oil to refresh and cleanse and equip me.

I thank you that you bless me to overflowing.

I thank you that your goodness and mercy will pursue me today and all the days of my life, and I thank you Lord that I am going to dwell with you – in your presence – now and through all eternity.'

This psalm just about covers the whole of life. We could probably draw on a different line of it every day, depending on what is happening during that day. Try starting your day with "Thank you Father that your goodness and mercy are going to pursue me (chase me down) today." – An amazing truth to dwell on at the start of each day.

Activation ...

There are so many wonderful scriptures to speak out like this. You will, I'm sure, have your own that are special to you. You could note some of them down in the space below.

Try putting your thanksgiving in front of these scriptures. It will stop you from just quoting them to yourself with a hopeful heart, and instead you will find that your faith is released as you speak them out with grateful thanks **to** the Lord. You will then find your confidence in His wonderful promises and in His love and care for you, growing day by day.

DAY 6 | Thanksgiving – My key to walking with the Holy Spirit

In Romans 8:14, we read that, 'those who are led by the Spirit of God are the sons of God', and I think that most of us who know that we are 'Sons of God' would probably like to 'do' better at being led by the Spirit. Learning to walk in the Spirit is one of those mystical and personal things, but I would like to share with you how 'thanksgiving' has played a huge part in that journey for me.

If we look at the time when Jesus was being led by the Spirit into the wilderness, we find that different words are used in the different gospels to convey what it was that the Spirit did, and what Jesus experienced.

In Matthew 4:1, for example we read that Jesus was 'led', or 'guided' even 'drawn' by the Spirit. While in the first chapter of Mark's gospel, a different Greek word is used, and is translated variously that Jesus was 'driven', 'compelled', 'forced' or 'impelled' by the Spirit into the wilderness. Words we may well identify with as part of our own walk with the Holy Spirit.

Now, let us imagine a fast flowing stream with a small log on it. As the log floats along it meets obstacles along the way: rocks, debris, or other twigs etc. The log depends on the flow of water to move it past the obstacles. Sometimes the water becomes forceful and 'drives', or 'compels' the log to move around the obstacle. At other times it looks as if the stream is gently leading, or 'drawing' the log, almost pulling it around the obstacle, while in other seasons, the level of the water rises and simply lifts and 'carries' the log over the obstacles. The main thing is that the log stays afloat, stays buoyant, because when it is buoyant it can be moved along by the flow of the water.

If we now imagine that the flowing stream is the Holy Spirit and that we are the log, we can see that moving with Him through the various challenges and joys of everyday life depends on us staying buoyant. As we go through a day, obstacles – difficult situations that arise, or hard decisions that have to be made, come our way, and we want to know what the Lord would like us to do.

We can help ourselves to stay buoyant in those moments *if we turn our hearts to the Holy Spirit in thanksgiving;* if we thank Him that He is with us and indeed within us, that we know He loves to guide us, and that He will lead us and carry us through any difficulties. We can thank Him that He will, if necessary, nudge, or even thrust us into the right path, and that He will give us wisdom, or insight where we need it as He draws us onwards.

Thanksgiving takes our eyes off of the 'obstacle' in front of us and our own ability to 'do well' and it tunes us in to the promptings of the Holy Spirit, however they might come. Thanksgiving in these moments can also remind us of His power and strength that will enable us to go forward. The truth is that He is our wonderful Helper and He delights to do just that.

Thanksgiving then becomes an expression of trust in our precious Counselor and Friend – the one Jesus said He would send as our 'on board' Helper. It helps us to become attuned to all the different ways in which He graciously leads and guides us, and we then find 'walking in the Spirit' to be the joy it was intended.

Activation ...

Today let us start a new lifetime habit of turning to the Holy Spirit with thanksgiving every time we have decisions to make, or challenges to face. Thank Him today that He is with you to 'guide', 'lead', 'draw', 'push', or 'carry' you forward into the right paths. Thank Him that He delights to lead you into paths of righteousness for His own Names sake. (Psalm 23:3), and that He will gladly give you wisdom as you ask with the thanksgiving that expresses your faith in His kindness towards you. (James 1:5, 6.)

DAY 7 | Thanksgiving that defeats anxiety

We know that Jesus specifically encouraged His followers with the words 'do not worry'. He said this with regard to our lives, food, and clothing etc. (Matthew 6:25.) 'Do not worry' is, in fact, a command, and in the Authorised Version we have the exhortation to, 'take no thought for your life', the implication being that **we can choose whether or not we take those anxious thoughts on board.**

Jesus goes onto explain that we can make that choice because we have a heavenly Father who cares for us and knows what we need, (verse 32). Jesus is here readily acknowledging that there will be many potentially worrying things in life that we will want to talk to Him about, but if our heart is filled with the truth that our Father cares for us, then how much easier will it be to resist the worries?

I don't know about you, but very often, for me, praying about worrying things and situations has in effect been telling the Lord what He already knows about my situation, and then 'worrying on my knees' for a bit while trying to persuade Him to do what I want Him to do.

At the end of a prayer time like that I am left with such questions as: 'Did I pray the right thing?', 'Did I pray fervently enough?' (James 5:14-16, feeds that one). 'Should I have fasted?' 'Did the Lord even hear me?' And at worst, 'I know He can, but does He want to help me?' or perhaps, 'Have I done something wrong that may hinder the answer?'

The apostle Paul has some wonderful advice concerning this problem, in his letter to the Philippians. He writes, 'Do not fret or have anxiety about anything, but in every circumstance *and* in everything, by prayer and petition (definite requests), **with thanksgiving** (my emphasis) continue to make your wants known to God.' Philippians 4:6,7. AMP.

The result of praying – talking to God – about these things and then **giving thanks to Him,** Paul tells us, is that God's peace will then 'set a guard' on, or 'garrison' our minds. This is good news indeed. Thanksgiving and God's peace can always trump fear and anxiety.

The reason for this is simple. The anxiety battle is in our minds. Fear or anxiety is caused by 'imagining' what might happen. It is in fact negative faith; 'faith' that the worst will probably happen, and no amount of reasoning will be able to reassure us. Nor can we know in our 'mind' that we have 'prayed the right thing in the right way'. If, however, we go back to Jesus' statement that we don't need to worry because our heavenly Father cares for us, we can see why 'thanksgiving' is so powerful in guarding our minds.

If, when we have made our requests to God, we begin to thank Him that He cares for us, that He has heard us, that He sees and knows what is best for us, and that it is His kind intention to do us good, (Romans 8: 28), then our mind is taken away from our problem **and** our performance in prayer, and is put onto Him, our wonderful Heavenly Father, and onto His power and His character.

Have a look at Isaiah 26:3 in the Authorised Version. It's a verse we often quote, 'Thou will keep him in perfect peace, whose **mind** is 'stayed' on thee: because he trusteth in thee.' I'm not familiar with the original language here, but I believe the word 'mind' has the same root as the word 'imagination'. So let us let the Holy Spirit fill our minds with those wonderful truths about God as we pray 'with thanksgiving'. Then our minds will be 'garrisoned' and no fearful imaginations from the enemy will rob us of our peace.

Activation ...

Today Lord I am asking you about ... (Something that is causing you concern or worry)

And I am thanking you that you have heard me and that I can leave these things in your hands, because you are loving, wise, kind and powerful.

(Don't worry if you have to repeat this more times before your faith rises up and peace comes. Worries tend to keep repeating themselves, and therefore so will your thanksgiving need to be repeated too.)

DAY 8 | Thanksgiving when we're in trouble

In Psalm 50:14,15 the Lord says to the psalmist, "Sacrifice **thank offerings to God, fulfill your vows to the Most High, and call on me in the day of trouble; I will deliver you, and you will honour Me.**"

We need to note here that these verses were written over a thousand years before Christ, when animal sacrifice was an extremely important element in the worship of God, and yet the Lord is saying to the Israelites that although He acknowledges their sacrifices of bulls and goats, what He really wants is their thanksgiving and the keeping of their vows to Him. Then, He promises, He will get them out of their troubles.

How often, when we are in a 'tight' spot, and feeling under pressure from one thing or another, do we 'up our game' a bit by making sure we:- Have a quiet time, pray harder, do some witnessing, or attend church meetings a bit more consistently. In our own way we try to earn God's help by pleasing Him in these ways. Our equivalent of sacrificing bulls and goats maybe?

The things mentioned here are all great ingredients in our growth as Christians, but sometimes they just might be making us feel more deserving of God's attention and help, when in fact what really draws His favour and help is something as simple as 'thanksgiving' in the moment.

The word sacrifice, in these verses, is significant because sometimes, when we are in difficulties, giving thanks is the last thing we want to do. For various reasons it sticks in our throats, or we feel hypocritical because we don't 'feel' thankful. Could that be a spiritual battle going on?

I do believe, incidentally, that our thanksgiving does give the devil a headache, but look how it is described at the end of psalm 50 in verse 23. We read, "**He who sacrifices thank offerings, honors me, and he prepares the way so that I may show him the salvation of God.**" Wow!

Who wouldn't give thanks on that basis? As my thanksgiving ascends to heaven it is like throwing up a pathway, a conduit, down which the power and presence of God can come into my life bringing salvation into my 'now'. I hope you can see what that picture conveys, or see in your own way, how powerful your thanksgiving can be in bringing the power of God into your situation.

It is good to remember here that we are not thanking God for the trouble we are in but that He will work it for good in our lives. Thanksgiving is about having the right words coming out of our mouths and hearts. It's about the confession of our lips saying that we believe God is 'for' us, that He loves us, that He is our Saviour, not just from our sins, but for life too.

In Deuteronomy 30:14 we read 'But the word is very near you, in your mouth and in your mind **and** in your heart, **so that you can do it**.' AMP. We can do this. We can make a choice to turn in thanksgiving to our God of deliverances and give Him glory as He helps us in all our troubles.

It goes without saying that the help He sends may be to get us out of trouble, or to give us grace and wisdom in our troubles. Either way, His help will be amazing, and you will find yourself drawing closer to the Lord Himself as you give yourself to 'giving thanks' in the moment of trouble.

Activation ...

Is there something happening in your life this week, where you can put this truth into practice? An area of life where you need to see the 'deliverance', or the 'salvation' of your God.

Write it down here. Then start giving Him thanks for this wonderful opportunity to see His loving hand at work in your life. Don't be in a hurry; some things take time and persistence!! And remember, once the deliverance comes, the unique opportunity that this particular situation presents to grow in faith in this way, will be over.

DAY 9 | Thanksgiving to silence the enemy

Yesterday we observed that our thanksgiving could give 'the enemy' a headache. Well! Of course we don't know if that can actually be done, but we do know that we can give him a profound headache metaphorically and spiritually speaking.

This is because the devil was totally defeated and disarmed at the cross, but since 'he is a liar [himself] and the father of lies and of all that is false,' John 8:44 AMP, his main weapon now is to convince us that God is not as good as He says He is, and that we are not totally accepted by Him. He does this work by whispering lies and half truths into our 'spirit ears' just as he did literally to Eve in the Garden of Eden. Genesis 3:1-5.

When we have a heart to walk with God and please Him, we are often particularly vulnerable to the devil's condemning half truths. 'You didn't do that right!' 'You could have done that better!' 'You have failed again!!' We can be going through the day, feeling OK about how we are doing and then Bam!! Something happens and we don't handle it well. We can feel like rubbish for the rest of the day. A far cry from the song we used to sing, a lifetime ago, which went, "I'm walking in faith and victory, for the Lord my God is with me."

Now we know that if we sin, or fall short in some way, but then we 'confess our sin, he is faithful and just to forgive us our sins and purify us from all unrighteousness.' I John 1:9. It's a done deal. The devil however has a great interest in reminding us instead, of how often we have done that thing, or how bad a witness we were, or that we really need to feel bad for the rest of the week in order to show how sorry we are.

So let's go back to giving the devil that metaphorical headache: and **yet again the answer is in our decision to break out into thanksgiving.** "Surely not!" I hear you say. "Isn't repentance meant to be a heavy-duty thing?" Well, actually no! In order to stop the devil from making us feel totally condemned, we need to understand that when he points out our mistakes and failures, he uses half-truths and takes us, spiritually speaking, to Mount Sinai and the law. The trouble is he's probably right about our failure, **but it's only half the story**.

When, however, the Holy Spirit convicts us of the same thing, **His** is a voice full of hope and He will always take us to Calvary, to the cross and He will remind us of the price that Jesus has already paid for our total forgiveness. We can silence the devil, (also known as 'the accuser of our brethren,' Revelation 12:10 A.V.) and our own internal sense of failure, by turning our hearts, our minds and our voices to thank Jesus very loudly for the complete and total forgiveness that He won for us on the cross.

I have met many Christians over the years who really believe that God loves them, but also feel that He is somehow disappointed with them, or fed up with their slowness to change. This fear then feeds into the lies of the enemy, making those lies hard to dismiss. The truth is that God 'knew' we'd be hard work!!! But He loved us enough to take us on. Furthermore, He has already provided, over two thousand years ago, on the cross, for every single sin that He knew we would ever commit. If I was an American preacher, I'd now be saying, "Do I hear a Hallelujah?!!"

Activation ...

If you are feeling a lingering sense of condemnation today for things in your past or present, sing, shout, or whisper your heartfelt thanks to Him. This will take your eyes off yourself and will bring great glory to Jesus in the heavenly realm. Jesus suffered all that pain and agony so that you can be completely free and stand before Him, clothed in His righteousness, to the amazement of the angels. Thank Jesus for the cross and all that He won for you there, and you can be sure that the enemy will not stay around for long with his accusations.

DAY 10 | Thanksgiving to silence the enemy. (Part 2)

In Romans 8:35, the apostle Paul asks the rhetorical question, 'Who can separate us from the love of Christ?' And then, in verses 37-39, he answers himself with the statement that nothing in all creation is able to separate us from the love of God that is in Christ Jesus our Lord, including natural disasters and spiritual powers. It's quite a declaration and worthy of much meditation.

While it is true that 'nothing in all creation' can separate us from His love, our own doubt and unbelief can certainly make us **feel** that God is a million miles away, or even that He has forgotten us and doesn't in fact love us in the way that Paul describes.

Here we have the second way in which the enemy seeks to defeat us: when he lies to us – and we listen – saying that God is not really as loving and good as He says He is. Satan makes us question, or even blame God for things that are hard, or difficult in our lives. It's a problem of our 21st Century mentality that can say: if God is good, loving and all powerful, bad things shouldn't be happening to me, His child.

The truth is that until we reach heaven, we will be living in a world profoundly affected by the 'fall' and therefore by the devil's activity. In our journey through life, the Lord promises His help and His presence, but calls us to walk by faith through much that we don't understand. The Bible, Old and New Testaments, deal with this issue and can help us to 'stand firm in our faith' if we will let the Holy Spirit teach us how things look from heaven's perspective. (See John 16:33).

The prophet Jeremiah often struggled in his ministry of delivering God's word to His people. Whilst being obedient to the call of God on his life, He suffered greatly and became somewhat perplexed with God for not 'covering' him, and for allowing him to be attacked spiritually, physically and emotionally.

In Jeremiah 15:15-18, he pours out his complaint to the Lord, finishing in verse 18 with the cry, 'Why is my pain perpetual and my wound incurable . . . ? Will you (God) be to me like a deceitful brook, like waters that fail and are uncertain?' AMP. His cry reveals a real questioning of God's faithfulness to him!

The reply (also taken from the Amplified Bible, verse19) is life changing for Jeremiah. God says, 'If you will return and give up this mistaken tone of distrust and despair, I will give you again a settled place of quiet and safety, and you will be my minister. If you separate the precious from the vile (that is CLEANSE YOUR HEART FROM UNWORTHY AND UNWARRENTED SUSPICIONS CONCERNING GOD'S FAITHFULNESS) you shall be my mouthpiece.'

May be it was after this encounter with God that he wrote the amazing words (that we have all sung in various settings) from Lamentations 3:22,23. 'The steadfast love of the Lord never ceases, His mercies never come to an end. They are new every morning. Great is your faithfulness.' (It is therefore good to read these verses in their context from verse 1 of the chapter.)

When assaulted by the murmurings of the enemy and the questioning in our own hearts, our weapon once again is **thanksgiving**. We can 'cleanse our hearts from those 'unworthy and unwarranted suspicions concerning God's faithfulness' as we thank God for the truths in Romans 8:35-39 written by the apostle Paul who, like Jeremiah, endured spiritual and physical abuse whilst doing God's work.

Activation ...

As you give thanks you will begin to 'see' the Lord's hand of love and faithfulness extended to you in your situation. You will silence the enemy and, like Paul, will be able to 'shout' ... 'No, in all these things I am more than a conqueror through Him who loves me.' Romans 8:37.

Have a go!!!

DAY 11 | Thanksgiving that enables us to receive

Over the last two days we have been looking at how, by giving thanks to God for the work of the cross and for our heavenly Father's unfailing love, we can help to protect ourselves from the wiles of the enemy. Thanksgiving focuses our hearts and minds on all that God is and blocks out the whispered lies of the enemy which undermine our faith. Today we will look at how thanksgiving not only shuts us out the activity of the enemy but, as importantly, it opens us up to receive from God all that He has for us.

In John 1:12 we have the very well known verse 'To as many as received Him He gave the power to become the children of God'. We often pray with people to 'invite Jesus into their lives' to become Christians. We encourage people to 'receive' their salvation as they **thank** Jesus for what He has done, to **thank Him** for dying on the cross for them and to **thank Him** that all their sins are forgiven.

 If we now read on in John Chapter 1 we come to another amazing part of the story. In verses 16 and 17 we read, 'For out of His fullness, we have all received one grace after another, spiritual blessing upon spiritual blessing, even favour upon favour and gift upon gift, for while the law was given through Moses, grace (undeserved favour and spiritual blessing) and truth came through Jesus Christ.' AMP.

The purpose of the amazing salvation that Jesus bought for us, is not only to have our sins forgiven but to become 'like Him' by being filled with His life. It is in order to be able to say with Paul 'I am crucified with Christ, nevertheless I live, yet not I, but Christ lives in me and the life I now live in the flesh I live by the faith of the son of God.' Galatians 2:20.

God's intention is salvation which leads to fullness. He wants us to be 'filled to the full measure of all the fullness of God.' Ephesians 3:19. Salvation is not a one off moment, but in Jesus own words it is a daily ongoing experience of the life of Christ pouring into us, and through us, by His Holy Spirit, John 7:37-39.

We now live our Christian lives by daily receiving of His power, presence and grace, and the way we receive is in the same way that we receive any gift; it is by thanking Him and enjoying what He gives us.

Watching a child can help us learn how to receive and enjoy God's gifts. When our grandchildren wanted specific Lego sets for Christmas, they would ask and keep on asking, (sounds like Luke 11:9!!) and when the gifts were given, they received their gifts with great joy and thankfulness and rushed off to build the latest acquisition. They did not hesitate, but ripped off the paper. They never stopped to ask, 'Is this OK? Can I really have this? I'm not sure I have been good enough!'

Receiving from the Lord, moment by moment, all that we need in order to live the kind of life to which He is calling us, is about 'knowing' what He is offering us as His sons and daughters, and then thanking Him for His gifts. Thanking Him for grace, favour, patience, peace, strength, courage etc. etc, whatever we need of the 'blessing upon blessing' for everyday of our lives.

Activation ...

Let's be childlike. (See Matthew 18:3) Let us tell Him what we need His wonderful indwelling Spirit to be for us and to impart to us. Then, as we thank Him by faith for those gifts, we will begin to experience them in our lives. Our thanksgiving will open up our hearts in faith and expectancy to receive and then enjoy all that the Lord wants to pour into us moment by moment, as we reach for the amazing goal – 'to walk in this world as He walked.' 1 John 2:6.

DAY 12 | Thanksgiving and enjoying the presence of God

There is much talk in our day about 'the presence of God', and we hear of those times and events when the Lord's presence becomes overwhelming for those who are present. We read of such an occasion in 2 Chronicles 7:1-3, when Solomon dedicated the temple he had built. We read that the glory of the Lord filled the house so that the priests couldn't even stand.

We may have heard people say that they 'felt' the presence of the Lord, for example, in a time of worship, and certainly we are living in times when the Lord is graciously giving us many manifestations of His presence. While we may look for those special times, we must not overlook the wonderful truth that the Lord is actually present with us **all** the time. I guess the clue is in His name: Emmanuel, God with us. And should that not be enough, one of the names God has given Himself is Jehovah Shammah, 'the Lord is there.' Ezekiel 48:30-35.

The truth is that while there are those wonderful moments in corporate or individual times of worship, when some say they experience the Lord's presence, for many of us it is in our everyday lives that we need to 'know' He is there, and so we can't therefore always rely on our feelings. A quick illustration is needed here about faith, facts, and feelings.

If you can imagine them following each other walking along a wall.

FEELINGS ⇨ FAITH ⇨ FACTS ⇨

All goes well as long as FAITH follows FACTS, but if FAITH looks behind and tries to follow FEELINGS, then FAITH will fall off the wall. Many of us get discouraged and can lose faith in the fact that God is present with us when we judge our circumstances by our feelings, or lack of them. The simple truth is: our feelings actually follow the facts that we are acting on. Perhaps that is why we sometimes 'feel' the presence of the Lord more in a time of worship, because we are spending time focusing on Him and 'declaring' the facts that we know about Him. Our praise and worship is coming out of our faith, and then we find that our feelings are following. We don't have to 'wait' until we 'feel' Him near. If we don't praise Him until we 'feel' it, because 'we must be real!!', then we may never discover His immanence in our everyday lives.

The writer to the Hebrews tells us in chapter 13:5 that God Himself has said, 'I will never leave you or forsake you.' In the Greek, the wording is actually a very strong triple negative. 'I will never, never, never forsake you.' This is a 'fact' we can actually step out on, letting our feelings follow.

I believe that in our ordinary everyday lives as we reckon on the fact that the Lord is present by His Spirit, and **thank Him** for that truth, we will begin to discern His presence in the moment. The good news is it doesn't have to be a long worship service. Even in the dedication of Solomon's temple, the song was very simple: 'They worshipped and **gave thanks** to the Lord saying, "He is good and His mercy (loving kindness) endures forever."

As we turn our hearts to the Lord by simply **thanking Him that He is with us, and that He is good and full of love** then, in whatever situation we find ourselves whether it be work, rest, or play, we will become aware of Him, His help, His guidance, His laughter, His travelling with us through the day. As we 'practice His presence' in this way, we will also begin to discern more and more clearly what He is saying to us and doing for us.

Activation . . .

Try thanking God that He is with you, regularly, throughout the day today in all the different circumstances in which you find yourself.

DAY 13 | Thanksgiving that increases our friendship with God and makes us whole

In Luke Chapter 17 we have the well known story of the ten lepers who met with Jesus and begged Him to have mercy on them. Their condition made normal life for them completely impossible, and so they appealed to Jesus to have compassion on them and to do something for them.

Jesus responds by telling them to go and show themselves to the priest. They go, and as they go they take a step of faith, a very significant one in that culture. They could have exposed themselves to the wrath of the clergy had they turned up leprous, but as they went they saw the healing taking place in their bodies. They were overjoyed but only one, we are told, turned around and came back to Jesus. He praised God in a loud voice, threw Himself at Jesus feet and thanked Him. This was no formality, it was heartfelt gratitude – and it came from the Samaritan.

Jesus response is twofold. First of all He asks about the nine who didn't come back. Clearly giving thanks matters to Him. This story makes me wonder sometimes, how often I have thrown up an emergency prayer and then taken the answer for granted, or attributed it to some natural circumstance that just happened to work out! I think, may be, that we often don't recognise God's hand in our lives, and we therefore miss some very important moments with Him.

We once had a Christian leader who suggested to us that the way in which we respond and receive one miracle probably affects the size of the next one and how soon it happens. I can't quote scripture and verse for that, but I think that what happened next, in the story of the ten lepers, gives us an indication that our leader may well have been right.

Jesus' secondary response was to address the grateful Samaritan directly. He gives Him an extra blessing, and a little bit of teaching on how faith works. He affirmed that his faith in obeying and starting off towards the priests was key to his being healed. How wonderful must that extra encounter with Jesus have been for that man.

As we give thanks to the Lord for things that He has done for us, we engage with our wonderful Jesus face to face. We continue the conversation with Him as we rejoice and give thanks to Him, and so we grow in our relationship with Him beyond just having Him meet our needs.

Many believe, and I do too, that when Jesus sent this man on His way for the second time, he left with a far greater measure of healing than the first time. In the AV the translators have used the expression, 'Your faith has made you **whole**'.

The Greek word used here is 'sozo', meaning saved, healed and delivered. I believe that every time the Lord answers our prayers His goal is not just to meet our needs but to 'make us whole,' to enrich our relationship with Him, and to impart more of Himself into our lives.

So let us not stint in our giving of thanks. Let us thank Him whenever we can, as effusively as we can. Let us thank Him for all His blessings, large and small, physical, spiritual and practical, knowing that as we do, we give glory to God. We will also be increasing our friendship with the Lord and His blessing on our lives, which in turn will speed us on to a greater measure of wholeness.

Activation . . .

What would more wholeness in your life look like? Thank the Lord for what He has already done (things big and small) and position yourself to receive more of that wholeness today.

DAY 14 | Giving thanks to let the world know about our God

We are living at a time when so many people don't actually know that there is a God who cares about them. It became very clear during the recent pandemic that the devil has done a good job of convincing people that God doesn't exist, with the result that few people know where they can turn when trouble hits.

Psalm 107 is an amazing psalm of testimony and praise to God for the many different ways in which He has delivered His people in times past. It begins, 'O give thanks to the Lord, for He is good: for his mercy endureth forever. **Let the redeemed of the Lord 'say so', whom he hath redeemed form the hand of the enemy.**' AV. (My emphasis)

Publicly thanking God for what He has done by 'saying so' is a wonderfully natural form of evangelism. Your testimony can open someone's eyes, Christian, or non Christian, to what they can have too, if they ask the Lord for His help in the different circumstances of their life.

I remember telling a University friend how the Lord was helping me and giving me peace during my 'finals'. His surprising reply? "I think I'm going to join your lot!!" By giving your testimony, thanking God for His help, His provision, His healing, His peace, or whatever else He has done for you, you can arouse curiosity in a friend or neighbour, opening a door to more conversation, or even prayer.

The world watches us and if we are living a thankful lifestyle we will have a ready testimony to share of things that the Lord has done for us. In Psalm 67:1, 2, the psalmist prays, "God be merciful to us and bless us and make his face to shine on us, that your ways may be known on earth and your salvation among all nations." Then in verse 7 he writes, "God shall bless us and all the ends of the earth will fear him".

When people 'see' and hear that God is at work in our life, they will know He is real and begin to 'fear' Him. Our thanksgiving and 'say so' will give God a lot of glory and may just save a life. So let us, 'the redeemed of the Lord', 'say so' – out loud – by giving our thanks to God for all the wonderful things He has done for us.

Activation . . .

Ask the Holy Spirit to remind you to share your testimony of all that He has done for you with Christians and non-Christians alike. Things will come more readily to mind if you are already thanking God for them yourself.

You could write a list below of some of those things that the Lord has done for you, thereby readying yourself for the opportunities when they come.

DAY 15 | Thanksgiving that enriches our relationship with the Lord

Over the years, I have seen the amazing power of thanksgiving to smooth glitches and upsets in our human relationships. When things are a little tense or awkward, saying 'thank you' to someone for something they have done, or for who they have been to you in your life, can do a great deal to restore a strained relationship.

This is true of children and parents, in both directions. It's true in church between leaders and led, or brothers and sisters. It's true between husbands and wives, friends and family, employers and employees and colleagues. Looking for something for which you can thank the other person and speaking that out, builds a bridge which then enables communication to flow more freely again. I think this is because when we show appreciation, we are honouring and valuing the other person and that creates a closer connection.

Obviously this appreciation needs to be genuine, but even parents who feel they are having to constantly correct a child, and so feel that a wall is growing between them, can find something for which to be grateful, and, by simply expressing appreciation for that one thing, they can lower that wall. It's amazing.

This dynamic seems to be true in our relationship with God too. When we read about Jesus with Mary and Martha around the time of Lazarus death, (John 11), Jesus appeared to be a frustrating, if not uncaring friend. We are told He deliberately delayed coming to them in answer to their request for help.

When He arrived, they obviously still loved Him and wanted Him there, but there is reproach and disappointment in their words and actions. Mary, the one who was commended by Jesus for sitting at His feet and 'choosing the good part.' Luke 10:42, didn't even come out to meet Jesus, and it felt like a rebuke as both Mary and Martha greeted Jesus with the words, 'Lord, if you had been here my brother would not have died.'

Jesus, however, had delayed out of love, not indifference, (verses 4- 6) because He had big plans for all three of them at this moment in their lives. He wept with Mary not because He was in grief Himself, but for the pain she was suffering. Pain that might perhaps have been a lot less had she been able to welcome Jesus in trust instead of in doubt.

As in our human relationships, when we don't quite 'get' what the Lord is up to, or indeed we feel abandoned, or let down by Him, let us not withdraw like Mary did initially, or put up a wall between us and God with our 'why' questions, but rather let us choose to welcome Him into our situation with thanksgiving and look expectantly to see what He's up to. He won't disappoint.

Again, as in our human relationships, we may not feel grateful for what is happening in the immediate, but we can thank Jesus, however bewildered we are feeling by our circumstances, that He loves us, died for us, and has redeemed us. In other words let's turn to Him in thanksgiving for the things we **do know**, thus helping ourselves not to put a barrier between us and God over the things we **don't know**, and **don't understand**, about what He is doing.

Activation . . .

If you are finding that hard to do you could use a song to give your thanks to Him, like the one written by Darlene Zscherch:-

Thank you for the cross Lord. Thank you for the price you paid.
Bearing all my sin and shame, in love you came and gave amazing grace.
Thank you for this love Lord, thank you for the nail pierced hands.
Washed me in your cleansing flow, now all I know:
your forgiveness and embrace.

I think He would love that, because He loves to 'hear our song in the night'. Job Chapter 35:10. That kind of song is very special to Him.

DAY 16 | Thanksgiving when we are being shaken

We are living in a media age, where we can get so much information about all the bad things happening in the world, that sometimes it feels like the news is just a display case for all that the enemy is doing. Famine, war, disease, poverty, natural disasters as well as all the evil humankind perpetrates on his fellow man. There is non-stop coverage if we want it.

It sometimes feels apocalyptic, and it can make us feel overwhelmed, insecure or very afraid. We can of course limit our viewing – a wise move no doubt -, but an even better antidote to fear would be to turn our hearts to the Lord and thank Him that **His** Kingdom cannot be shaken and that we are a part of that Kingdom.

At the end of Hebrews 12, in verses 26-29, we read that God is going to shake the earth and the heavens so that only those things which cannot be shaken will remain. It's a quotation from the prophet Haggai. The writer then goes on to say, 'Therefore since we are receiving a Kingdom that cannot be shaken, **let us be thankful** and worship God acceptably with reverence and awe, for our God is a consuming fire'.

It is interesting that the word 'apocalypse' in these days, is often used synonymously with the disasters from the book of Revelation. The word 'apocalypse' is actually the Greek for our English word 'revelation'. The full title of the last book in the Bible is actually 'The Revelation of Jesus Christ'.

It is in fact a revelation, or unveiling, of the Lord and His ultimate victory over all that the devil can and will do to thwart Gods plan of salvation. The book ends with the marriage of the Lamb to His blood bought bride. It is a 'revelation' not to scare us but to encourage us. Chapter 22:16 reads 'I Jesus have sent my angel to give you this testimony for the churches.' The end of the story is that God wins!!!

We have all heard of the phrase, and probably used it ourselves, "I **can't thank you enough.**" We associate it with times when we are extremely grateful for something. Something lifesaving literally, or metaphorically speaking. It's a phrase the Lord brought to mind, I believe, for this meditation. Maybe it's a phrase we need to use when it feels as if our whole world is being shaken.

We have a kingdom that cannot be shaken, and as we turn and thank the Lord for His presence, His promises, and His care for us, He will reveal Himself to us in all the shaking. He will show Himself to be our faithful deliverer in all our troubles. Paul in Romans 8:31-39 covers just about every trouble that could come our way, when he declares that 'in all these things we are more than conquerors through Him who loved us.'

Activation . . .

In these shaking times let us turn to Jesus and say, **"Lord I just can't thank you enough** that in all these things you are with me and will never leave me, and that nothing can separate me from your love. Neither death nor life, neither angels, nor demons, neither the present nor the future, nor any powers, neither height, nor depth, nor anything else in all creation will be able to separate me from the love of God that is in Christ Jesus my Lord".

Now that's security!!

DAY 17 | Thanksgiving that brings contentment

In 1 Timothy 6:6, the apostle Paul writes to the reader that 'Godliness with contentment is great gain.' AV. What a challenge his words are to us in the 21st century. The spirit of the age, the **'atmosphere' in which we live, is designed to make us discontent in every area of our lives:** how we look, what kind of home, kitchen, lifestyle we have, what kind of job we have etc. etc.

I would say that this is one of the enemy's current insidious, and often unrecognized, attacks on us. It comes through the advertising that constantly bombards us, through every medium it can; through the barrage of messages that propagate dissatisfaction and discontentment with every aspect of our lives. It gives us the sense that in order to be happy we need 'more' and 'better' in all aspects of life, including our friends and relationships. We can find ourselves very busy fighting off a generalized sense of dissatisfaction and discontentment.

This 'atmosphere' can also seep into the very fibre of our being and make us discontent with ourselves, and ultimately with who God has made us to be, and how He has made us. This kind of discontentment must so grieve the heart of God for it clearly matters to God that we know how wonderfully He created us. Look at His reaction after He had created the world and finally humankind. Genesis 1:31 tells us 'God saw **all** that He had made and it was **very good**'.

The Psalmist in Psalm 139:13,14 'gets it'! He says 'I will give thanks to you for I am fearfully and wonderfully made: wonderful are your works, and my soul knows it very well.' NAS. How powerful is that? He is agreeing with God that He did a good job. That agreement through thanksgiving must so bless the heart of God. It can also, I believe, bring about a great deal of acceptance and contentment into our hearts as we rejoice with God over our lives and who He has made us to be.

Psalm 139 goes onto talk about God knitting us together in the womb, and in these days when we have so much information and even living pictures about what is happening in those nine months in the womb, let us never stop being amazed at the incredible and intricate design and working of our bodies.

If in any doubt, look up the amazing facts about your blood, and what it does every day, as it courses through you veins. Or think about your skin and its ability to protect, repair and renew. We could go on; so given that there is so much staggering information available to us, let us thank Him for our amazing bodies every day we live.

If we can do this we will take our eyes off of the kind of 'perfection' sold to us by the airbrushed pictures of the ideal man and woman, delivered into our homes daily and hourly. Our thankfulness to God will also rob the enemy of his ploy to make us unhappy with ourselves and ungrateful for the life God has given us.

The same truth also applies to our personality and circumstances. Later in verses 16 and 17 of the Psalm 139, David says: God 'knows the days ordained for us' and 'precious to me are your thoughts'. I like the foot note in the NIV which indicates this could read, 'precious **concerning me** are your thoughts.' God thinks about me; He knows my personality, my upbringing, and the path of my life. It's a path unique to me. No one else has the opportunities I have today and every day of my life to love and serve Him, amongst those I meet in my life situation.

By thanking Him for our bodies, our personality, our life, and our circumstances, we are expressing our agreement with Him, and thereby releasing ourselves from discontentment.

Activation ...

Consider spending ten minutes today specifically thanking the Lord for who you are, who He has made you to be and your circumstances in life. Thank Him for your unique body, your unique personality, your gifts and talents, your brain, your emotions and all the care that He has taken in making you, you!

DAY 18 | Thanksgiving and living a Godly life

If we think of a Godly life as one that manifests the character of God, we can see that the fruit of the Spirit, listed for us by Paul in Galatians 5:22, encapsulate the 'God-like-ness' our new life in Christ should portray. If we are living in a 'Godly' way we will see love, joy, peace, patience, kindness, goodness, faithfulness, gentleness, and self control, increasingly on display. What an incredible list, and how seemingly unattainable it can sometimes seem to be!

The picture Paul paints of the opposite, 'ungodliness,' is not pretty. In Galatians 5:19 his list depicts the 'acts of the sinful nature' (flesh in the older translations). This list does not just include idolatry, witchcraft and sexual sin but also hatred, jealousy, envy, selfish ambition, dissensions, and anger; things to which we can perhaps all relate in some measure.

There are, for example, multiple ways in which we can be unkind, or impatient during the day, gossipy or lacking in self control, and since kindness, patience, goodness and self control are fruits of the Spirit and attributes of our God, how can we best help ourselves to cooperate with the Holy Spirit to produce that good fruit in our lives? In other words – **How do we live a 'Godly' life?**

In Romans Chapter 1:28-31. Paul traces the spiritual and moral decent of humankind into a people who are gossips, slanderers of God and who invent ways of doing evil. People who are senseless, heartless and ruthless, who become futile in their thinking, with their hearts darkened.

He points out that the decline started with a failure to give thanks. 'They neither glorified Him as God nor **gave thanks to Him'** (verse 21). So if the lack of thanksgiving is the start of the decline into ungodliness, may be here, perhaps, there is a clue for those of us who may not have gone down the route described in Romans 1, but who struggle, at some point during most days, to keep our lives manifesting the fruit of the Spirit, as described in Galatians 5:22. Those of us who want to live Godly lives.

That clue is I believe 'Giving Thanks'. If refusing to honour God and thank Him started the downward spiral described in Romans 1, then the opposite must be true. If we travel through the day in a spirit of gratitude, we will find that our thankfulness releases the Holy Spirit from our innermost being and the fruit can grow. The key to staying in a flow of life where we are manifesting those fruit and displaying Godliness is, therefore, to stay in a thankful mindset.

If we honour God with our thanksgiving in a situation we will counteract the temptation to think ungodly thoughts (i.e. getting irritated), which can then progress to ungodly beliefs (this person is a waste of space), and then actions (shouting or being rude to them). For example someone annoys you, if you start thanking God for them, or even for His love for you, that angry thought is more likely to die than become an angry decision, leading to an angry action, or angry words.

As we go through a day with our hearts filled with gratitude, we will find ourselves less prone to judge, to criticise, to be unkind, or impatient and we will be less likely to lack self control when we need it. If we should hit a challenge along the way and find ourselves tempted to react badly, choosing to give thanks is very often the thing that will enable us to overcome that temptation and live more like Jesus. Also, in practical terms, the pause that choosing to give thanks creates is likely to reduce the pressure to respond negatively.

This all makes perfect sense if we see that godliness is really just a life of letting the Holy Spirit flow freely through us, producing His fruit in our attitudes, thoughts and actions.

Activation ...

Look for an opportunity today to put in a pause by giving thanks when you feel a negative reaction to someone, or something, rising up.

DAY 19 | Give Thanks Generously

I was impressed this morning by the simplicity of the statement 'GIVE THANKS'. **Giving** thanks is different to 'being thankful, or even having a heart of gratitude. It's an activity, a choice, and wonderfully it is something everyone can do.

We don't need money, education, status, or any particular skill to do it. It is in fact one of the first things many parents teach their children as soon as they can speak. It is so simple! How wonderful of the Lord to give us a way of connecting with Him and blessing His heart that is so easy. 'Our Thanks' are something each one of us can give Him just by making a choice.

How we do it also matters to God, because the next thought that came to me was the statement in 2 Corinthians 9:7 which says, 'Each man should give what he has decided in his heart to give, not reluctantly or under compulsion for God loves a cheerful giver'. So God loves **cheerful** giving -no surprise there!

I imagine we have all been in the excruciating situation where a child has been forced to thank us for something they really didn't want. It's not great to be on the receiving end of thanks given grudgingly. It's no surprise then that God loves freely given thanks, even when it's a sacrifice.

A song that I heard in the 1970's still rings in my head. It captured for me the essence of those verses in Corinthians. It was sung by some very merry singing nuns!!! The two lines of the chorus went . . .

God loves a cheerful giver. Give it all you've got,
He loves to hear you singing when you're in an awkward spot.

I don't think it would make the Christian top twenty today, but, in that it links giving thanks with giving generously and freely, it probably should.

Generosity is at the heart of our God. There were twelve baskets of food left over after the feeding of the multitude, (Luke 9:17). There were six stone water pots filled with 20 gallons of wine each at the tail end of a wedding!

(John 2:6). There is forgiveness for ALL our sins, however many and however big they are. And let's not forget to mention the fact that our very generous God created a universe that is just teaming with extravagance. Our creator, it seems, just couldn't stop Himself creating, and so He gave us a world to live in which displays a vast array of sights and sounds, colour and taste for us to enjoy.

Jesus said, "Give and it will be given to you. A good measure, pressed down, shaken together and running over." Luke 6:38. Paul understood this aspect of His God when, after encouraging his readers to give cheerfully, he wrote that, 'God is able to make **all** grace abound to you, so that in all things, at all times, having all you need, you will abound in every good work.' 2 Corinthians 9:8. That is a lot of 'alls' plus one 'every'!!!

Our wonderfully generous God is just straining to respond to our joyfully given thanks, with a further outpouring of His love and grace. So let us **'Give Thanks'** today, big time, for whatever we can, big or small. Indeed, let us give our thanks freely and generously to our exceedingly generous God, and don't then be surprised at the blessings that may well be coming your way.

Activation . . .

Try it!!!

DAY 20 | Thanksgiving that grows our appreciation of the Lord and others

We attended the funeral of an old friend yesterday, and in the course of preparing a short appreciation of him for the service, Mark, my husband, got out some old photos of holidays and times shared together, and we fell to reminiscing about our friendship of some forty years.

We had always enjoyed and valued our friendship but as we looked back, and with the benefit of hindsight, we realised what a truly precious thing that friendship had been, and how much it had enriched our lives. It made me wish that I had been more grateful at the time for that friendship, more intentional in my thanks to God for having this person in my life, and also more appreciative to the person himself.

Have you ever noticed that we often only fully appreciate something, or someone, after it, or they have gone, or we have moved on ourselves? This can be true of so many things in life: a job, an aspect of our health, a church, friends, family members, even our house, or location. In many ways the recent Covid pandemic – where familiar things were shut down, or taken away – highlighted this for us.

I think now, that being thankful at the time and in the moment is the answer to growing in our appreciation of someone, or something. It can work like the unwrapping of a parcel in the children's party game 'Pass the Parcel'. As we give thanks for one thing, another layer is unwrapped and something else surfaces for which we can be truly thankful.

For example, when a friend does you a favour, or helps you out, you can say thanks and move on quickly, or you can 'unwrap' the favour a bit further. As you thank them for the help they have given, you realise there is a kindness here for which to thank God. Then it 'dawns' on you that this kindness has cost this person (time, or money, or both). You realise they are generous too. As you thank God for that, you see another layer of blessing, God has

44

given you a brother or sister who cares about you enough to serve you in this thing, and before you know it, the value you place on that person and their friendship has grown.

Giving thanks to the person and to God for that person, stops us from taking for granted what is there in our life. Even more it stops us from slipping into entitlement – the sense that we have a right in life to all the good things, and good people, God sends our way.

Thanksgiving also keeps us from ruminating on the negatives of a situation, or the flaws in a person's life. Giving thanks enables us to savour the good in both things and people, to grow in our appreciation of them, and as an added bonus, we become a nicer person to be around!!

Paul so often started his letters with thanks to God for his friends in the different places he had ministered, the most notable to me being his thanks for the Philippians. 'I thank my God for every remembrance of you, always offering prayer with joy . . .' Philippians 1:3, 4, (NAS.) His heartfelt appreciation must have so warmed the hearts of those Philippians, in that he didn't just pray for them but that he was deeply, frequently thankful to God for them.

Activation . . .

Spend some time today thanking God for the people in your life, and let the Holy Spirit unwrap for you the treasures in those people that you may be taking for granted. This practice could become transformational – for you and your friends, and an important part of your everyday life!

DAY 21 | Thanking God for the people who we find difficult or who challenge us

Yesterday, we talked about how thanksgiving can enhance our appreciation of the people in our lives, and thereby enrich our friendships. I believe thanksgiving is also important, for the difficult and challenging people in our lives. They too can be a blessing to us, if we allow the Holy Spirit to be our helper on our journey to 'walk as Jesus walked.' 1 John 2:6

Jesus consistently displayed the fruit of the Spirit throughout His time on earth, and this wasn't just when He was surrounded by His followers and people who loved Him. We know that He was often challenged and threatened. He is the One 'who endured such opposition from sinful men.' Hebrews 12:3. Yet, as we observe Him in diverse and challenging situations throughout the gospels, we are amazed. He stands head and shoulders above everyone, even at the end as He is being crucified.

For us, if we can embrace it, difficult people shine a light on where we need to grow. They expose where there are difficulties for us in manifesting the fruit of the Spirit. When we come across someone who causes us to behave, or think, in ways that are ungodly, our natural reaction can vary. We can get very discouraged with ourselves, we can blame them, or we can decide to avoid them. Alternatively we could choose to thank God that **this person,** has brought to light an area in our life where we need to grow in our new nature in Christ in order to become more like Jesus.

In Galatians 2:20 Paul says, 'I have been crucified with Christ, and I no longer live, but Christ lives in me. The life I live in the body, I live by faith in the Son of God, who loved me and gave Himself for me.' Colossians 2:6 says 'So then, just as you have received Christ Jesus as Lord, continue to live in Him, rooted and built up in Him, strengthened in the faith as you were taught, and **overflowing with thankfulness.**' Verse 9 continues, 'For in Christ all the fullness of the deity lives in bodily form and you **have been given the fullness of Christ**, who is the head over every power and authority'.

We have all seen the bracelets WWJD. It's a helpful reminder, but wearing such a reminder to DO What Jesus Would DO is not going to help if it just means I grit my teeth and 'try to be nice', or 'try' to produce the fruit of the Spirit. Instead, Colossians 1:27 tells me that it is Christ in me who is my hope of glory. It is also therefore Christ living in me, by the Holy Spirit, who is my hope of responding to a situation 'as Jesus would'.

So if, when I am facing a difficult situation with someone, I can give thanks for them, this can be a means of releasing the Holy Spirit within me to bear His fruit; to produce longsuffering, kindness, wisdom, strength, self control, in fact every grace in whatever form I need it. This will be by His Spirit in my spirit. It's the life of Christ within that is my peace, my joy, my ability to walk though the situation as Jesus would. Grace is not 'dropped' on me from above, but rises up from my spirit as I am filled by, and overflowing with, the Holy Spirit.

I can thank God for the situation and **also for the person** because they are the means He has chosen to work grace into my life in this particular season, and in this particular way. They are a gift to me, helping me to grow. Suddenly they are not the 'enemy' but someone God is using to cause me to draw more deeply on the wonderful 'Counselor, Helper, Intercessor, Advocate, Strengthener, and Standby,' – the Holy Spirit.' John 14:26 AMP.

Activation . . .

Once again – try it!!!

DAY 22 | Thanksgiving when we are weary

In Isaiah 40:28-31, we read that the Lord, the creator of the universe, never 'grows tired or weary', and what's more: 'He gives strength to the weary and increases the power of the weak'. This new strength and power is promised to those who 'wait for the Lord', or 'wait upon the Lord'. A mysterious phrase, but a promise we often claim in a weary moment without always understanding what is involved.

'Waiting on the Lord' is not like my childhood memory of waiting for a bus to get to school, hoping it will come, but knowing that it might not. This verse has an air of certainty in it, a promise for us from our loving heavenly Father who, we are told, in verse 28, not only doesn't get weary, but also has understanding 'that no one can fathom.'

The encouragement to those who 'wait upon the Lord' is that their strength will be renewed or 'exchanged.' (AMP). The verse then goes on to talk of them mounting up on wings like eagles. What a beautiful image of strength and power – one that is worthy of further consideration.

The eagle, like any bird of prey, likes to nest, or perch, high on a cliff so that it can 'wait' to catch a thermal. When the bird senses a thermal it will then launch out and soar effortlessly on outstretched wings to hunt for prey. The eagle will ride that thermal, and gain height, without needing to flap its wings. Should the bird see a storm or turbulence ahead, it will soar above the storm, keeping its eyes on the sun, rather than exhaust itself by flying through it.

So how do we 'wait on the Lord', and how does that help us to 'mount up on wings like an eagle'? Well! Thanksgiving is not written into these verses, but I do believe it is a key for us, if we are to learn the art of 'waiting on the Lord'. It can therefore play a fundamental part in the 'exchange', or 'renewal' of strength that we are needing when we are feeling worn down and weary. Waiting on the Lord has that sense of stopping and giving Him our full attention. When we are weary it can be our cue to stop and to take the time to sit back, to take a deep breath, to 'spread our spiritual wings' and to catch the thermal of God's love.

Giving thanks to the Lord; that He is with us, that He is close, that He understands our weariness, that He cares, that He loves us deeply, not only causes us to stop, but also to turn our eyes onto Jesus, and thereby 'spread our wings' and begin to rise up in our spirit on the thermals of His love.

Just like the eagle rises as it gazes at the sun, stopping to thank the Lord in this way is like lifting our eyes to our 'Son'. It helps us to catch the thermals of God's love as we look at the amazing care and love for us Father, Son and Holy Spirit have. We slow ourselves down, and take time to drink it all in. We then find our spirits refreshed and rising up. Energy and strength will be renewed because we know that weariness is not just physical, but emotional and spiritual too. Waiting on the Lord can help us in body, mind, soul and spirit. The Holy Spirit is interested in replenishing us in all these areas.

The main thing we must learn to do is ignore the enemy's lies. He will tell us, "You don't have time for this." "You don't have the time, or energy, to 'wait' on God." Now since he is the father of lies we can be sure that the opposite is true. We cannot afford **not** to wait on God, but we must learn to do so, by turning our heart to Him in thanksgiving and catching the thermals of His love. We will then discover that His promise is true and our strength is renewed.

Activation . . .

If you are feeling weary begin to wait on the Lord. Start gently with kindness towards yourself. Put aside just ten minutes to 'wait on the Lord' as described here. Some instrumental worship music may help you to begin your thanksgiving, and then you may well find you want to take longer than the time you have allowed yourself, so make some allowance for that too!

DAY 23 | Thanksgiving and the angels

Yesterday we saw how waiting on the Lord can help us to renew our strength. Today we are looking at another source of supernatural strengthening – the angels. In Hebrews 1:14 we are told that angels are 'ministering spirits sent to serve those who will inherit salvation'. They come to us as He commands, bringing blessings from heaven where they spend time worshipping around the throne of God. Revelation 5:11,12.

If you look in a concordance at the word angels you might be amazed, as I was, at the amount of angelic activity in the Bible. Talking of angels can either seem a little far out to our 21st Century rational minds, or it can be taken over by the kind of 'New Age' talk of angels which is unbiblical and unhelpful. In addition sometimes we Christians spend more time worrying about what the devil and his angels are doing on the earth, than appreciating what magnificent allies and helpers we have on our pilgrimage through life in the angels who serve our God.

I am always encouraged by the possibility, gleaned from Revelation 12, that when the devil was thrown out of heaven he only took a third of the angels with him. That means the good ones outnumber the bad! Two to one!!!! Apart from that fact, we need to realise that our angel helpers serve the omnipotent God, while the others serve an already defeated devil. It's good to remember that truth when we are feeling overwhelmed by what seems to be enemy activity.

Throughout the Bible angels have appeared at various times and seasons to help people. For example when Hagar was desperate Genesis 16:7, an angel of the Lord 'found' her and helped her. In Numbers 22:24, an angel came to stop Balaam from making a big mistake. In Genesis 31:11-13 an angel came to Jacob in a dream to tell him it was time to leave Laban and to go home. Luke tells us in the first two chapters of his gospel that angelic activity was prolific around the birth of Jesus. And in the early church, it was an angel who rescued Peter from jail. Acts 12:7,8.

Sometimes the angels were seen; sometimes they came in dreams. Sometimes they just looked like ordinary men, and were even entertained by people who were unaware of who they were, Hebrews 13:2. Even in our own lives I suspect that we just don't know how often we have been ministered to, or protected by, angels. We have no way of knowing how often we have been guided by unseen angels, or stopped from doing something unwise. We often don't know, like Elisha's servant in 2 Kings 6:15-17 that, 'those who are with us are greater than those that are with them.'

I love the line in the song 'Blessed Assurance' which goes, – '**Angels descending bring from above, echoes of mercy, whispers of love**'. Of course the Holy Spirit leads and guides us, but what about those times when some verse, or card, or encouragement has surfaced for you at just the right time? I believe there is probably far more angelic activity involved in incidents like this and in the unseen protection of our lives than we can possibly imagine.

So back to our 'Thanksgiving' theme! In the song quoted above, before the line about the angels we read 'This is my story, this is my song. Praising my Saviour all the day long.' We said in an earlier meditation that 'thanksgiving is the language of heaven', so it follows that it is the language around which the angels feel most comfortable.

I believe the angels will always be there at God's bidding when we cry out for help, but I'm also thinking that as we praise and thank God they delight to join us of their own accord. I don't have chapter and verse for this, but I believe our thankful hearts and voices, as we go through the day, welcome the angels into our world, and into our circumstances.

Activation . . .

Look up the word 'angels' in a concordance and be blessed as you see all that they do in the bible, and that they can therefore do for you. Thank God for them and for all the things that they have done for you that you probably know little about. You can also, I believe, by having a thankful heart make them more welcome in your life and so enjoy all the blessings that they bring.

DAY 24 | Giving thanks in advance!

Every morning when we get up and look at the day ahead of us, we face the prospects of things that need to be done, people to see or speak to, and choices to be made. Some of those things will be enjoyable, some we will do easily and some will present us with fresh challenges, but as we start each day, we would love to feel that we will live it well, bringing glory to Jesus, and that we will sense His 'Well Done' at the day's end.

I guess none of us, at the beginning of our day, face things the size of the daunting task that Moses had when he was commissioned to take the people of Israel into the Promised Land. Like Moses, however, we may well want to say to God, as we face the day with its 'unknowns' and challenges, 'If your presence does not go with me, do not send me up from here'. Exodus 33:15.

At the start of his commission, Moses had previously asked the question "When the Israelites ask me the name of this God who has sent me, then what shall I tell them?" Exodus 3:13,14. God gave him that wonderful answer, "I AM who I AM. This is what you are to say to the Israelites: I AM has sent me to you."

The Amplified Bible expands that statement to, 'I AM who I AM and what I AM, and I WILL BE WHAT I WILL BE.' J.D. Douglas in the New Bible dictionary explains: 'This name signifies the active presence of the person in the fullness of the revealed character.' In other words (my version!) God is saying "Moses, I am actively present and involved with you, with whatever of my manifold attributes you need in any given moment."

The good news for us is that we know that our God is with us, He is our Immanuel, and has said 'Never will I leave you; never will I forsake you.' Hebrews 13:5. So we too can say 'The Lord is my helper; I will not be afraid.' Hebrews 13:6. We can face anything in any day, knowing that the Lord is with us, and that the indwelling Holy Spirit, our helper, is with us too.

What would happen if, as we scanned each day in the morning, we thanked God for all that He was going to be for us during that day? This thanksgiving would actually be a confession of our faith in the Lord's promise to be all that we need Him to be. Our personal great I AM. We could thank Him in advance that He will give us the wisdom we will need for situation X, the patience we will need in situation Y, and for the courage, love, endurance, and grace etc. for the unexpected and unanticipated.

We could thank Him that He will help us with our choices in the use of our time, and that 'as our day is, so will our strength be'. Deuteronomy 33:25. We could thank Him that He will provide whatever we will need, for whatever is coming our way, through our new life in Christ.

Is this just presumptuous, or a real expression of faith? Well, when we get on a bus and pay our fare in advance, we do so because we believe the bus is going to take us to where it says on the front of the bus. I believe that in the same way, **thanking God in advance** for all that we need Him to be for us in the day ahead, is in fact believing that; **i) He is who He says He is, ii) That He will do what He says He will do, and iii) That He will be with us, and for us, and all that we will need Him to be.**

Activation . . .

Why not start your day with thanksgiving in advance, thereby 'banking', or building up, your faith for the grace to draw on throughout the day. Then you can walk through the day with Jesus, enjoying His presence, drawing on Him in each situation, and giving even more thanksgiving for His enabling presence as you go.

DAY 25 | Thanksgiving and the Joy of our Salvation

In Isaiah 12 we have a beautiful passage. It is the song that was going to be sung by God's people, after He had redeemed them. A song which we, who have been redeemed by Jesus' death and resurrection, can fully embrace and enjoy today.

In verse 3 we are told 'With joy you will draw water from the wells of salvation.' In this picture we are introduced, firstly, to the idea that salvation is like a well, and secondly that we can actually draw up more and more of the water in it, with joy.

A well in those days would have been a hole, dug deep in the ground, reaching down to an underground water table, or water course. Having a well that didn't run dry would be vital. Clearly the 'wells' of salvation described in Isaiah were not going to run dry, as drawing water from them was going to be an unending source of great joy.

When I was 'saved' at a huge evangelistic meeting in 1966, a very dear lady, who acted as my 'counsellor', asked me if I had 'assurance of Salvation'. I hadn't a clue what she was talking about. I just knew that I had started a new life, and this time, God was in charge. Fifty six years later I most definitely have 'assurance of salvation,' and I am also still drawing water from the incredible 'well' of salvation' that opened up for me that day.

Sometimes when we've been on the Christian road for some time, we can get so that we feel we've "got it under our belt". We know and understand all the basic truths and know what the Christian life should look like. We've done 'church' for many years, and we have our salvation sorted. We can at this time be in danger of losing 'the joy' of our salvation.

The problem can be that we are thinking of salvation as a set of doctrines and behaviours, when in fact, it is a love affair; the most incredible relationship ever, with the Lord and Creator of the whole universe, our most wonderful Redeemer! His love is so high, deep, and wide that we can never fully 'comprehend' it (Ephesians 3:16-19); and so is His incredible plan of salvation. It is so much more than we can ever imagine.

In these days God is preparing a bride for His Son; (Revelation 21:9-11), and I believe that He would love for us to be sharing His excitement and expectancy as we increasingly realise all that His deep, deep love for us means both now and in the days ahead, and then for all eternity.

So how do we stay enthralled? How, in fact, do we keep drawing fresh water from the never ending water supply that is this 'well' of salvation? Well one way is to be intentional in thanking God for what you know He has given you, and done for you. As you thank the Lord for what you **do** know of His love and work in your life, He will open up to you fresh revelation from old and "well known" truths. There will also be fresh understanding of the depths of His love, which Paul says we can never fully comprehend.

Activation . . .

Thank Him for what you know you have in your 'new life in Christ', and then ask Him to take you deeper, higher, further on, into all that His death on the cross bought for you, and all that walking in 'newness of life' in Christ means. (Romans 6:4). Giving thanks for these things is like putting your bucket down the well again, to draw up more of this wonderful living water and I am sure that if you do so, it will bring you great joy.

DAY 26 | Thanksgiving in Trials

James' letter to the church starts by encouraging the readers to 'count it pure joy' whenever they 'face trials of many kinds' James 1:2. In another translation the encouragement is to 'consider it **all** joy, when encountering various trials' RSV. It's a challenging exhortation to get our heads round in the 21ˢᵗ century, where our life goals are more often directed towards happiness and comfortable living.

James, however, inspired by the Holy Spirit, encourages us to count these trials as 'pure joy' because of all the amazing things that they will produce in our lives. They will test our faith, which, in turn, will help us to persevere, and somehow perseverance, we are told, will make us mature and complete, not lacking anything (verses 2 and 3). Quite amazing!

When we consider our circumstances in the midst of a 'trial', we don't always know the cause; whether our circumstances are caused by an attack of the enemy, a consequence of living in a fallen world, the result of someone's sin, or even the consequence of our own sin, or choices.

We can spend much time agonising over how we came to be in the middle of such a trial, and then find ourselves wondering "How should I pray; for deliverance, or for grace?" We try to think through how we should handle the trial, and we can also find ourselves battling negative emotions like fear, anger or condemnation.

Whatever the source of the trial, we know from Hebrews 12:1-12 that struggling against sin and enduring hardship are both used by God to train and discipline us. The wonderful thing about that is that this is a sign that we really are His children (verse 7). Like James, the writer to the Hebrews also points out that God's discipline might not be pleasant, but it will yield beautiful fruit in our lives if we allow ourselves to be exercised by it. (verse 11)

We know that the Lord in His love, and by the power of His Holy Spirit, will take any trial, from any cause, and use it to mold us and mature us. We also know that He will probably be able to do that faster and more quickly if we offer our thanks to Him in the midst of the trial, thereby making a way for Him to come and do His wonderful transformational work in our hearts and minds, and deep in our spirits.

We might not know where the trial is coming from, and we might not understand it at the time, but as we intentionally 'count it pure joy' by thanking God in our difficult circumstances, we will travel through it, and find ourselves being changed to be more like Jesus day by day. Thanksgiving will also guard our hearts from the discouragements, or the perplexities that work against us.

In Hebrews 12:2, we are encouraged to 'fix our eyes on Jesus' who suffered for the 'joy set before Him.' Part of that joy was seeing the likes of you and me come into His family, (Isaiah 53:10,11.) So now that we are **in** His family, let **us** count it 'pure joy' that He is working in us through our trials, and that He loves us enough to make sure that we are being 'changed to be like Him,' little by little, through it all. (2 Corinthians 3:18.)

Activation . . .

Take a moment today to 'fix your eyes on Jesus' by turning to Him with thanksgiving for what He suffered for you. Then thank Him also that He is with you in whatever trial, or testing you are currently facing.

DAY 27 | A second reason to 'Give Thanks' in times of trial

James in his letter to the church encourages the believers in Christ to 'consider it pure joy whenever they face trials of many kinds'. I think that there are two main reasons for giving thanks when we are facing trials. We looked at the first yesterday, and it's the reason James himself gives. We thank the Lord because He will use the time of difficulty to do good things in us and for us.

It seems to me that the second reason for being thankful for the trials is because any trial that we face causes us to call on the Lord for His help. In other words, it becomes an opportunity for us to discover more about who God is, and who He wants to be for us, on our journey through life.

In some ways this is very obvious. For example I will never know, or prove that God is my wonderful 'Provider', unless I need Him to provide for me. Abraham found this out (Genesis 22:14), when, at a time of great testing, God provided a ram for him to sacrifice in place of his only son.

Throughout the Bible we see how people discovered the character and nature of God through their times of challenge. David clearly proved God in his shepherding days and that became His testimony, written for us in Psalm 23. When he was on the run from Saul, God became his 'high tower' (Psalm 144:2) and his 'refuge' (Psalm 27:1).

When we're in trouble we can read, to encourage ourselves, all that God did for the heroes of faith. We find parallels in their stories to our own, and it releases faith in our hearts to reach out to God for ourselves. Hagar, for instance, discovered God to be the 'one who sees' when it felt like no one else was looking, or caring. (Genesis 16:13). How wonderful is that – to know, that when we are in a time of trial that no one else seems to fully see, or understand, God does?

I love the King James translation of 2 Chronicles 16:9 'The eyes of the Lord run to and fro throughout the whole earth, to show Himself strong in the behalf of them whose heart is perfect towards Him' The Lord wants to be more than a story in a book to us, He wants to actively come into our situations and show Himself to be our El Shaddai, our God All Mighty.

If the enemy sends us a trial, or if life throws up some difficulties, we can thank the Lord, even sometimes in our brokenness, because through that trial we will be able to 'know' more of our God. Know more about who He wants to be for us, His love for us, and His power in our lives in a way that may be no other circumstance would allow.

Every one of God's names denotes something of our Lords character. So as you face your next difficulty, thank Him, draw close to Him, realising that this could be a moment, or a season, in your life where you will find Him in a new way. Let us thank Him for our trials with the excitement and anticipation of what we are going to see the Lord do and be for us; and what He is going to demonstrate to us of His amazing self.

Activation . . .

You could list below some of God's wonderful names, so that in a time of trial you will be ready!!

DAY 28 | Thanksgiving that helps us to remember

In the Old Testament one of the things about which God gave strong instruction, was that His people were to consistently remember Him and all His acts on their behalf. In Deuteronomy 6:7, for example, we read how the Israelites were encouraged to keep talking about the commandments to their children. God was also concerned that they should not forget Him when everything was going well for them, and so He told them to 'be careful that you do not forget the Lord who brought you out of the land of slavery'.

To help them to remember His help in crossing the Jordon, the Israelites were told to place twelve stones, one for each tribe, at the river, (Joshua 4:20-24). When the next generation inquired about the stones, they were to tell them that they were placed there as a tangible memorial that the Lord had enabled Israel to cross on 'dry ground'. They were there as a constant reminder so that they and future generations, 'might always fear the Lord your God'.

Another example comes in 1 Samuel 7:12. Samuel took a stone and set it between Mizpah and Shen. He named it 'Ebenezer' (stone of help) saying "Thus far has the Lord helped us." In doing this God gave the people a visual aid, lest in the future they forget the amazing deliverance from the Philistine armies that they had just experienced.

It's a problem we humans have; we forget so easily, but I believe that 'thanksgiving' is a gift that helps us to remember. As children, we were always encouraged to thank aunts and uncles for birthday and Christmas presents. Often by the time the letter came to be written, we had forgotten what it was that we had been given. Writing that letter helped us to remember and appreciate again the gift that had been given.

These days we have many things that help us to remember, like the photos of a holiday, or a souvenir we have kept. We take numerous videos of our children and grandchildren, wanting to hold on to delightful memories. My mother in law always kept a diary, and could look back to remind herself of events that happened years before. In the same way thanksgiving is a very important way of reminding ourselves of all that God has done for us.

To look back over a day, a month, a year, or even over a past season, with thankfulness, seals those memories in our hearts. Taking time to say 'Thank You' and naming specific blessings is so important. Sometimes it is even good to sit down and write God a 'Thank You' letter. Or keep a 'Thank You' diary of all the good things, big and small, that the Lord has done that week.

Psalm 103:2 AMP, says 'Bless the Lord, O my soul, and forget not [one of] all His benefits.' We need to keep the thanksgiving flowing for both the spiritual and the practical blessings because, as we keep remembering with gratitude, our faith and confidence in the goodness of God builds, as does the maturity we need to handle the next challenge that may come our way on our journey through life.

Jesus Himself at the last supper, after He had given thanks, told His disciples to break the bread in remembrance of Him, (Luke22:19). Interesting then, that some parts of the church, now call this the Eucharist. Eucharisteo, meaning 'to give thanks'. Jesus knew that we would need a constant reminder of His sacrifice for us. So, yes, let us break bread with thanksgiving in our hearts, and let us also thank Him intentionally for all the other blessings that we experience in our lives too.

Activation . . .

Is it time to write a 'Thank You' list, or a 'Thank You' letter to God for this past week? For some that could be in the form of a poem or song, even a painting. Remember God loves our creativity as well as our gratitude!

DAY 29 | Thanksgiving in times of disaster

I am aware that, sometimes, an encouragement to 'give thanks' can seem somewhat trite, or glib. This is especially true when someone is facing huge losses, or personal disaster, as is the case when people lose jobs, money, loved ones, direction, or just hope for their future.

Habbakuk found himself alive at a time of great turmoil. God was going to bring judgement on His people, and He was going to do it by using a very ungodly nation, the Babylonians, and so Habakkuk had many unanswered questions going around his head. He foresees the day of distress and trouble coming and 'decay crept into his bones'. He went all 'trembly' and weak. Habakkuk 3:16.

Then, out of nowhere as it were, he makes this amazing declaration recorded for us in Habakkuk 3:17-19. 'Though the fig tree does not bud, and there are no grapes on the vines, though the olive crop fails and the fields produce no food, though there are no sheep in the pen and no cattle in the stalls, yet I will rejoice in the Lord, I will be joyful in God my Saviour'.

Just amazing!! Let's be clear here. This is an agricultural society with no supermarkets, no welfare state (as we know it) and no defense against this invading army; He is foreseeing and describing total ruin. Yet he determines to find 'joy' in God. His name Habakkuk, means 'the one who embraces'. How wonderful is that? This man is able to 'embrace' God and His purposes in the midst of impending disaster.

In a recent communication about the difficulties our nation, indeed our world may soon be facing Jonathan Bugden, a friend, was encouraging God's people to 'brace themselves from a place in God's embrace'.

So how do we 'embrace' God and all He wants to be for us in times of disaster? How do we even start to 'rejoice in the Lord'? Yet again, I believe it starts with our 'thank you'. These times are times when we need to 'dig deep'. Habakkuk says he will be joyful in his Saviour. We need to remember more than anything else what the Lord has done for us on the cross, and as we do we can start to find His 'embrace' by thanking Him for our salvation.

We can thank Him for what we have been saved from; thank Him for undeserved mercy and grace, for forgiveness and for His suffering on our behalf. We can also thank Him for His unchangeableness, for His steadfast love for us. Lamentations 3:22. We can thank Him that He will never leave us or forsake us. Hebrews 13:5. It's a time for digging out all the promises of God, and reminding ourselves who He is and who He wants to be for us, regardless of our circumstances.

I remember one time feeling very low and shaken. It felt like I was sinking in doubt and confusion. Mark (my husband) said "you need to find a rock to stand on." By which he meant, find an unshakable truth about God to stand on – to speak out and meditate on. I did and it 'stopped' the slide.

Being able to say, "I don't know what is going on, but this I do know 'The eternal God is my refuge and underneath are His everlasting arms.'" Deuteronomy 33:27, and being able to 'thank Him' that he will be with us, with His comfort, even in the dark valley, Psalm 23:4, is vital. These are the truths that we can thank Him for, and these are the truths that will 'kick start' our rejoicing in the Lord.

Tomorrow we will look at what happens next for Habakkuk!!

Activation ...

Have you got an unshakeable truth about the Lord, a 'rock', on which you can stand in times of trouble. Write it down below, and remind yourself daily of it with thanksgiving. Then ask the Lord for another (and another!).

DAY 30 | Thanksgiving, Joy and Strength

Today we are going to look at Habakkuk's declaration in Habakkuk 3:17-19. We are going to look at his intention to 'be joyful in God', despite the impending disaster about to befall his nation, and at the amazing changes that this decision – to 'rejoice in the Lord' – brings to his life.

Let's be clear. Habakukk makes his declaration in the face of the possibility of complete agricultural failure, and therefore economic disaster in his homeland. Even if, he says, there are no grapes, figs, or olives, no crops in the fields and no animals left, i.e. no nourishing food or meat to eat ourselves, or with which to trade, "I will rejoice in the Lord."

Then he shares the result of this momentous decision. He says 'The sovereign Lord is my strength; he makes my feet like the feet of a deer, He enables me to go on the heights.' verse 19. The Amplified Bible expands that last statement as meaning, 'He makes me walk, and not stand still in terror, to make spiritual progress upon my high places, (of trouble, suffering, or responsibility).'

His decision to 'rejoice in the Lord' brings him strength, not just to keep going, but to make progress in the face of the catastrophe about which he is prophesying. We too can discover that joy and rejoicing strengthen us, not just in the good times but also in the very bad times.

It's interesting that neuroscience, research into the activity of our brains, can now show us that joy, laughter, singing and even just thinking positively all help to 'lift our mood' by releasing helpful chemicals into our brain. Incidentally, this also agrees with the scripture, written some thousands of years ago, that 'A cheerful heart is good medicine, but a crushed spirit dries up the bones.' Proverbs 17:22.

We even talk about these things in physical terms. We describe feeling 'weighed down' by a worry and then, when it is dealt with, it is as if the 'heaviness', or the 'burden', is lifted. People talk about 'jumping for joy', because, even in the natural world, joy is a recognised energizer.

Paul knew about the power of rejoicing, and encouraged the Christians he was writing to with the words 'Rejoice in the Lord always, I will say it again: rejoice.' Philippians 4:4. {An easy text to remember!!}. Paul felt so strongly about this that he didn't mind repeating himself – and this from a man who was in prison, who had suffered greatly for his faith, and was expecting to be martyred.

The Apostle Peter, writing to Christians who were being persecuted for their faith, also encouraged them to 'rejoice in their faith' even though 'now for a little while you may have to suffer grief in all kinds of trials.' 1 Peter 1:3-8. He talks about the joy that is theirs because of their faith, and the 'inheritance that can never perish, or fade, kept in heaven for them.' Here again, 'joy' and 'rejoicing' in the Lord was going to give them the strength they would need to get through a time of suffering.

We, like those early Christians, can thank God for all that He has done for us in saving us from our past and our sins. We can thank Him for all that He has won for us; our future with Him in heaven. We can also thank Him even in a time of trial, for all that He gives us in the present, and that we are 'seated in Christ in heavenly places', and 'sealed with the Spirit'. Ephesians 1:13 and 2:6. This kind of thanksgiving then becomes the key to rejoicing 'in the Lord' and thus finding the strength to walk with Him through very difficult times.

Activation . . .

Like the psalmist make rejoicing a choice today . . . *This is the day that the Lord has made;* ***we will rejoice*** *and be glad in it.* Psalm 118:24.A.V.

. . . and may be you can 'kick start' that rejoicing with some thanksgiving for the past, the present and the future blessings of your salvation.

DAY 31 | Giving Thanks and Finding Gods' Will

Throughout this month, we have been looking at the various situations where 'giving thanks' can make a powerful difference to our lives. As we look back, we can see that our thanksgiving is in fact giving expression to our faith. If we are not feeling a great deal of 'faith' we can, by choosing to intentionally 'give thanks', actually 'pull ' ourselves, as it were, into a place of faith, in the various different life situations in which we find ourselves.

As we consider the transformational power of thanksgiving, we can then understand why Paul encouraged the church in Thessaloniki to 'be joyful always; pray continually; <u>give thanks in all circumstances, for this is God's will for you in Christ Jesus.</u>' 1 Thessalonians 5:16 -18.

This encouragement from Paul can especially apply when I am wondering what the Lord's will is, or what He wants me to do, or say in a certain situation. From these verses, I know that whatever the 'overall will' of God for me might be, in the immediate His will is always that i) I stay joyful, ii) I pray, and iii) that I give thanks in the situation facing me.

I can stay joyful because I know He is with me, and committed to helping me. I can also pray and give thanks, because I know that He loves me, and will give His wisdom to me unstintingly, if I ask for it without doubting. I can know this because James writes, 'If any of you lacks wisdom, he should ask God, who gives generously to all without finding fault, and it will be given to him. But when he asks, he must believe and not doubt.' James 1:5.

Those doubts that he mentions could be about my own worthiness to be guided, about my own ability to 'hear' the Lord, or even about the Lord's willingness to show me the way ahead. Thanksgiving can demolish, or at least minimize, my unbelief, and it will give voice to my faith that He will give the wisdom and the guidance that I need.

If it is wisdom for a big decision in my life, I may need to wait a while for the answer. If it is to know the Lord's will in the course of my day to day life, for example to know His wisdom in a difficult circumstance, or an awkward situation, then I do need to understand that His wisdom may not come in the way I expect, or through the 'direct line' that we all would love to have with heaven. God is creative in the different ways that He guides us, and through whom He reveals His will. We need to be attentive!

Our thanksgiving is our expression of trust that wisdom **will** come, and a heart of thanksgiving opens us up and gives us the grace to receive the beautiful wisdom that we need. We can recognise God's wisdom because it's different to worldly wisdom. God's wisdom is always, 'pure, peace loving, considerate, submissive, full of mercy and good fruit, impartial and sincere'. James 3:17.

So whenever you find yourself wondering what to do, or what the will of God is for you, there is no better way to start your conversation with the Lord than by asking for the guidance you need, and then by giving thanks to Him. Thank Him for the situation, for the choices before you, thank Him that He is with you, and then thank Him as you wait expectantly for His wisdom to come.

Activation . . .

Is there a current situation where you need and want to know the Lord's will and wisdom? Intentionally give thanks in this matter and keep mixing thanksgiving with your prayers and thoughts about it, and stay thankful in expectation that His wisdom will come.

DAY 32 | Thanksgiving that shows we agree with God

Throughout the Bible, the life of 'faith' is often referred to as 'walking with the Lord.' In 2 Corinthians 5:7-9, Paul tells his Christian readers to remember that 'we walk by faith not by sight' and that we should 'have as our ambition ... to be pleasing to Him' (RSV.) Enoch was a man who 'walked with God' and was clearly so pleasing to God as he walked 'in faith', that he didn't die but God, we are told, just 'took him.' Genesis 5:22-24.

So how can we be sure that we are walking with God in a way that is pleasing to Him? What does it mean to 'walk by faith and not by sight'? We can get a major clue from the prophet Amos, when he asks the rhetorical question, 'Can two walk together, except they be agreed?' Amos 3:3 (AV.) Agreeing with God, is then, a key to walking closely with Him.

When I was a student, I had a wonderful African Christian friend who preferred to make her own delicious food rather than eating in the canteen. On occasions she would invite me to join her, which I would gladly do. Her food was delicious! One day she got quite angry with me, because, apparently, every time she invited me, I would reply – like a well brought up English person should – something like, "Well thank you. That would be nice, but are you sure?"

She had finally had enough of my English 'politeness' saying that she found it insulting, because it was throwing doubt on her integrity. That is to say, she wouldn't have asked me if she didn't mean that she wanted me to share the meal. She wasn't just asking because she felt she had to. What she wanted to hear was my unequivocal, 'Thank you. That would be lovely.'

My 'thank you' would be my agreement with her, without any expression of doubt, or of needing additional reassurance. It would show her that I believed her offer was genuine. In other words my 'thank you' would enable us to 'walk together' as we shared that meal. I would be expressing my faith in her offer, and then I would receive the meal. My 'thank you' would also give her the joy of knowing that our friendship was sure.

I believe that there is a longing in the heart of God, for a people who will walk with Him in agreement. And before you protest that you always 'agree' with God, just think how many times you have sought His reassurance that He loves you; that He's still okay with you, or even that you haven't already wrecked His plans for you today, or this year!

God wants us to 'take for granted' what He has already 'granted' us. Not taking **Him** for granted in a careless way, but in a faith filled way that expresses our trust in Him, and in what He has said. So we are going to spend the next few days looking at some things that God says with which we really need to 'agree'.

We want our faith to bring joy to His heart, and we are going to signal our agreement with Him by our thanksgiving for some of the many things He has already granted us, His children; things about which we often have unacknowledged doubts. This could be life changing!!!!

Activation ...

Maybe a good way to start these next few days would be by telling the Lord that we are sorry for the times we have not taken Him at His word, but have sought His reassurance for things He has already given us in Christ.

You might like to ask the Holy Spirit to highlight one or two of those things to you right now, and write them down in the space below, and then specifically give Him thanks for them.

DAY 33 | Thankgiving for His love

Over the next couple of days, we are going to learn how to 'delight God's heart' by taking Him at His word, or, as the Bible calls it, 'walking by faith' – which is of course the only way to live as a Christian, as 'without faith it is impossible to please God.' Hebrews 11:6. God is so delighted when we believe Him wholeheartedly, refusing to live by our feelings, or what our enemy, 'the father of lies.' (John 8:44), says. He is so pleased when we agree with Him, and 'walk' according to His word, that He cannot help but pour blessing into our lives.

Yesterday, we wrote that we can express our agreement with God by our unequivocal 'Thank you'. We know, however, that when He speaks a truth to us, either directly from the Bible, through a song, or a word given to us (Ephesians 5:19), we often receive it with 'a divided heart'. One part of us believes God, but often deep inside, doubts, fed by the lies of the enemy, prevent us from agreeing with God wholeheartedly.

So today let us look at the whole question of God's amazing love for us. Many of us still find it hard to believe that God 'really, really loves us'. We know He died to save us, and that there is no greater love than that (John 15:13), but sometimes it is hard to know deep down inside that the Father loves us with the same love He has for Jesus. And yet it's true! Have a look at John 17:23. The truth is there is only one quality of love in the Godhead: pure, lavish, personal, unconditional love, and all that pure love, because of our faith in Christ, is now fully flowing incessantly, and relentlessly, towards and over you and me. (1 John 3:1)

I remember one time, while in a meeting, singing a worship song, I sensed that that the Lord was saying that He wanted me to change the words from 'I love you, Lord' to 'You love me, Lord'. It felt all wrong, a bit proud, even presumptuous, but when I did faith was released deep inside me, and joy too, as the significance of what I had just confessed with my mouth sank in.

It reminded me of the scene, in romantic movies, when the hero finally declares his love to the heroine. After he has gone, she bounces round the house, singing, 'He loves me; he loves me; He really, truly loves me.' Before his declaration she had just been hanging onto whatever clues she could find, as to how he really felt about her. Now if the hero could also see her joy he too, I think, would be delighted knowing that His beloved now believed him.

I once witnessed a minster of some years receiving the precious truth of God's love as if for the first time. Someone was praying over him and, as he did, he sang the simple children's chorus, 'Jesus loves me this I know, for the bible tells me so. Yes, Jesus loves me. Yes, Jesus loves me. Yes, Jesus loves me. The Bible tells me so.' As he prayed and sung these words over and over again, the love of God broke into this minister's life in a new way, and he wept with joy at the truth he was receiving in his heart.

To say 'I thank you God, from the bottom of my heart,' sharpens my faith and stops me playing around with doubts and unbelief. It stops me entertaining those sneaky thoughts, that "perhaps God loves X –who seems to be so blessed and doing so well – more than me," or the thought that "He really can't love me much now. I've made such a mess of today."

So, let us break our agreement with **any** of these sorts of lies, and decide to enthusiastically agree with our very loving and patient Heavenly Father. Let us **thank God unreservedly for His unconditional love**. As we thank Him we will also be declaring truth over ourselves, and as we do that, we will bring great joy to Jesus. We will be 'walking' with Him, in agreement about His love. A love that He has already, fully and conclusively, demonstrated on the cross. We will then be getting closer to being 'fully believing believers'!!

Activation . . .

Today, turn to the Lord and say, 'Thank you Jesus, that you really, really love me.' Say it as often as you can, and whenever you remember. I know it sounds almost too simple, but let's do it. For Jesus sake, come into agreement with Him as you thank Him, and so let this foundational truth sink into parts of you that it has never reached before!

DAY 34 | More about God's Love

Before moving on to today's meditation, I was going to add a post script to yesterday's thoughts. However now I am thinking that we need more than a postscript. In fact we need at least another day to focus some more on thanking God for His amazing love. I believe it is **strongly** on God's heart, that in this 'stormy' season His people should come to know the depth and quality of His love, because He is forming a bride who knows how much she is loved, and who will therefore be able to return that love.

Many beautiful hymns have been written about God's love over the years. Often they speak of the love of God as a huge ocean. For example 'Here is love vast as the Ocean', and 'Oh, the deep, deep love of Jesus, vast, unmeasured, boundless free, rolling as a mighty ocean, in its fullness over me.'

Today, I believe, God is releasing fresh revelation about His love through many of the worship songs being written at this time, and my postscript to yesterday's thoughts was going to be some of the words from Jonathan David Helser's song, 'Find Me'. It's an expression of his longing to know that vast ocean of love deep within.

'Find me grateful. Find me thankful. Find me on my knees ...,'

''Till the breath of your hope fills the depths of my soul, and all I know is I've been found by love.'

Paul too had a passion that the Christians around Ephesus would grasp how big the love of God was towards them. He knew that grasping that truth would take supernatural revelation, even for those first century Christians, and so he prayed a wonderful prayer for them.

'I kneel before the Father ... And I pray that you, being rooted and established in love, may have power, together with all the saints, to grasp how wide and long and high and deep is the love of Christ, and to know this love that surpasses knowledge – that you may be filled to the measure of all the fullness of God.' Ephesians 3:17-19.

Wow, God's love is beyond anything we can imagine, and in grasping something of its dimensions, we may become '[a body wholly filled and flooded with God Himself]!' Ephesians 3:19 AMP. This is clearly a prayer for more than just 'head knowledge', or intellectual assent.

So, where does the power to grasp this love come from? The answer is through the Holy Spirit Himself. Paul, writing to the Romans, in the context of trials, says, 'Hope does not disappoint us, because God has poured out His love into our hearts by the Holy Spirit, whom He has given us.' Romans 5:5

I personally love the AV version of that verse, which talks of the love of God being '**shed** abroad in our hearts by the Holy Ghost.' When I think of the word 'shed', I remember what happens when a lorry accidentally 'sheds' its load on a motorway. That word 'shed' depicts to me a total release of all that the lorry was carrying.

Activation . . .

Today, continue saying 'thank you Jesus, that you really, really love me' and then add – 'and thank you Holy Spirit, that you will show me how big that love is, as I open my heart to receive from you. I thank you, and invite you to 'shed' all that you are carrying of the love of God for me, into my heart today.' Amen.

DAY 35 | Love for one another

Yesterday we were looking at how the Holy Spirit loves to 'shed the love of God abroad in our hearts' and at how we can open our hearts and receive that love by saying 'Thank you' to Him. Today we are looking at the truth that God not only wants a 'bride' who truly believes she is loved, but also a 'body' on earth whose members love each other.

In the last few verses of John 17, we are privileged to hear Jesus' prayer to the Father for His disciples, *"I have given them the glory that you have given me that they may be one as we are one: I in them and you in me. May they be brought to complete unity to let the world know that you sent me, and have loved them even as you have loved me."* Unbelievably Jesus is looking for the same love and unity among His people, as there is between Him and the Father.

Peter of course heard Jesus pray this prayer, and encourages some later disciples with the following words. '**Love one another deeply, from the heart.**' 1 Peter 1:22. He knew that Jesus prayer was not just for the twelve, but was God's heart for all His family, so he passed on these words in his letter.

"What?!!" I hear you say, "Impossible!" Well, yes. That is true, humanly speaking, it is impossible for us to love all God's children 'deeply from the heart'. This is probably because the family of God is comprised of the likes of you and me! We are all saved sinners, on our way to being transformed into His likeness. We are all, in fact, a work in progress and not always very loveable.

Our reaction could be similar to Zerubbabel's, when the Lord spoke to him about rebuilding the temple. The local Persian officials were causing trouble by complaining to King Darius, and he may well have thought, "I have no idea how we are going to do this." A similar thought might go through our minds when it comes to loving our brothers and sisters in the same way that Jesus loves us. Zechariah gave Zerubbabel the answer. One we may recognise. 'Not by might nor by power, but by my Spirit,' says the Lord Almighty. Zechariah 4:6.

It's the answer, I think, that the Lord would give us today. We truly love only by His Spirit within. We have been thanking the Lord for the Holy Spirit's work in showing us how much the Lord loves us, now let us also thank the Holy Spirit for His help in enabling **us** to love others, knowing that Jesus also said "'Whoever believes in Me . . . , streams of living water will flow from within him." By this He meant the Spirit, whom those who believed in Him were later to receive.' John 7:38,39.

The apostle Paul significantly places 1 Corinthians 13, **the** chapter on love, between two other chapters well known for their teaching on the gifts of the Spirit. The truth is that 1 Corinthians 13 actually describes the kind of love that God Himself pours out on us. It is therefore only possible to love like this as the power of the Holy Spirit fills us, and then flows out from us in the gifts and church life described in 1 Corinthians chapters 12 and 14.

If we take the words from 1 Corinthians 13:4-7 and add some 'thank yous', we can receive and release the love of Christ, by the power of the Holy Spirit. We can grow to be more like Jesus, loving as He loves. So pray through these verses slowly, using something similar to what I have written below, and let us delight God's heart by allowing His Holy Spirit to grow us on our journey towards the goal of loving each other as He loves us.

Activation . . .

I thank you Holy Spirit that the love you are releasing through me is patient, and is kind. I thank you Holy Spirit that the love you are pouring through me towards others doesn't envy or boast, and it is not proud. I thank you Holy Spirit for your love within me that is not rude or self seeking. I thank you Holy Spirit that the love you 'shed' abroad in my heart is not easily angered, and does not keep a record of wrongs. I thank you Holy Spirit that your love within me for others does not delight in evil, but rejoices in the truth, and I thank you dear Holy Spirit that the love you are releasing through me always protects, always hopes, and always perseveres.

DAY 36 | Thank Him for your robe of righteousness

Today we are continuing our theme of giving thanks as a way of expressing our agreement with, and total acceptance of, all that the Lord has done for us. One of the things we need to thank Him for is the fact that we are totally forgiven. Being grateful for the forgiveness He has bought for us on the cross helps us to deal with any condemnation that comes when we are aware that we have failed or sinned.

We 'know' in our heads, from Isaiah 53, how Jesus' sacrifice on the cross paid completely and totally for all our sins and failings, but somehow we can still 'feel' easily condemned and guilty. This is not surprising since we have an accuser, who delights to keep us from enjoying all that Jesus won for us. Satan wants us to live with feelings of condemnation, because they do not honour Jesus' sacrifice in any way. In fact they can bring us into disagreement (i.e. unbelief) about Jesus complete and finished work on the cross.

The good news is that Jesus didn't only die to pay the price for our sin, He also gave us the gift of His righteousness in exchange (Romans 5:17). Paul tells us He has also become our 'righteousness, holiness and redemption' (1 Corinthians 1:30). Now, so far as God is concerned, we are 'clothed' in His righteousness, and Jesus' death has justified us before the throne of God, once and for all.

The fact is our 'robe of righteousness' comes straight from heaven (Isaiah 61:10). The Lord paid for it with His blood and put it on us when we asked for forgiveness and received Him into our lives. That robe of righteousness is not removed every time we sin, otherwise it would be off and on all day, almost like living in a changing room in Marks & Spencer!!

We know we still sin. John in his first letter to the churches said that we'd be deceiving ourselves if we 'say we have no sin'. The answer, he says, is to confess it, not hide it 'because God is faithful and just and will forgive those sins and purify us from all unrighteousness.' I John 1:8,9. We do still however have an enemy, 'the accuser of the brethren', Revelation 12:10, who does not want us to live 'condemnation-free'.

Let's see how God deals with Satan by looking at what the prophet Zechariah saw in one of his visions. He saw Joshua, the high priest of the time, being accused by Satan. He was standing in 'filthy clothes' (sounds like you and me from time to time.) Zechariah then hears this, "The Lord rebuke you, Satan! The Lord who has chosen Jerusalem rebuke you!" Then the Angel tells those who are standing by: "Take off his filthy clothes." He then turns to Joshua and says, "See I have taken away your sin and I will put rich garments on you." Zechariah 3:2-5.

We so need to hear those words spoken to us personally. So now imagine that you are a beggar, and you've been offered a beautiful robe in exchange for your rags. Would you not say 'thank you', clean up, and put it on? Some of us need to do that with God, and see His delight as we accept the robe of righteousness with joy and gratitude, and without protest that we are not worthy, because although it's true that we aren't worthy, Jesus has chosen to make us worthy.

I love the line in Jarod Cooper's song 'Majesty' that goes – *'In Royal Robes I don't deserve, I live to serve, Your Majesty'.*

Activation . . .

Today thank Jesus for the cross, that His sacrifice was total and sufficient for all your sin. Then, say a big 'Thank You' for the wonderful robe of righteousness that He paid for with His life. Wear your robe with joy, and any time you feel condemned or unworthy turn to the Lord and thank Him again for that robe. He will be so pleased, and the devil will be silenced.

Let's do it!!!

DAY 37 | Thanksgiving that magnifies the Lord

In the early days of the charismatic movement, we used to sing a song based on the AV translation of the Magnificat – Mary's song. It started with words that always puzzled me 'My soul doth magnify the Lord . . .'. I understood the sentiment but I didn't think you could make God any bigger than He was. So why magnify Him?

The penny dropped recently when I realised that when we magnify something, we don't make that thing bigger, but we put a lens in front of our eyes in order to see better all the intricate detail not seen by the naked eye. If we think for example about viewing an insect or flower, magnifying it is actually about enlarging the image of what is there in order to see it more clearly. Magnifying something enables us to see it in all its detail and magnificence.

Magnification can work negatively too. Worry for instance – something at which we are often very good – magnifies our problems. As we ruminate on and fret about our difficulties, they can seem to become larger. By focusing on them, we can see them as quite overwhelming.

I was encouraged recently by a quote from Mark Buchanan's' book 'The Rest of God'. It said, *'Thankfulness is a secret passageway into a room you can't find any other way . . . It allows us to discover the rest of God – those dimensions of God's world, God's presence, God's character that are hidden, always, from the thankless.'*

Yes, I thought, that is what I am realising. Giving thanks magnifies the goodness and kindness of God. Thanksgiving acts as our magnifying glass to help us see those dimensions of God's character that are hidden to the ungrateful eye.

During these days when one crisis after another seems to hit our world, the news media often place that bad news under the microscope. We must therefore, while not burying our heads in the sand, choose carefully what **we** are magnifying.

As we continue with our theme of thanksgiving, let us take some time to 'magnify' an aspect of God that we so need at this time, and let us give Him our heartfelt thanks that His 'goodness and mercy will follow us all the days of our lives.' (Psalm 23:6)

It is worth noting that the word 'follow' in this last verse of Psalm 23 is not the 'sneaking after you in the shadows' kind of following, nor is it the kind of following that arrives too late!! It is rather the very active 'pursuing after you' kind of following. Goodness and mercy are pursuing you and you won't ever be able to shake them off, because it is the declared activity of the Spirit of the Lord Himself.

Activation . . .

Let us thank God for this amazing truth about His love and intention towards us. If we can look back, recognise and thank Him for all the ways in which this has been true in our lives in the past, we will be putting a magnifying lens on Him, and so be building our faith for the future. We'll know that however uncertain life looks, **He** will be there in it with us, with His goodness and mercy in pursuit.

*Mark Buchanan 'The Rest of God', Nashville: Nelson 2006

DAY 38 | Thanksgiving that defeats fear!

We hear a lot these days about the high levels of 'anxiety' that people are experiencing at this time. I think that what we call 'anxiety' is what the Bible would call fear, and we know that the Bible is full of exhortations, in both the Old and the New Testaments, not to be afraid – to 'fear not'.

When we read verses in the bible about 'not being afraid' it is never because there is nothing to worry about. No! The encouragements to 'fear not' usually come with a 'because' – a reason. For Joshua for example it was because, 'the Lord is with you.' Joshua 1:9, while for Jehoshaphat, because, 'the battle is the Lords'. 2 Chronicles 20:15. For the psalmist it was because 'He is my refuge and my fortress.' Psalm 91:2.

From these scriptures we can see that the antidote to fear is always God's presence. It is God Himself being there for that person in some way. Jesus Himself gave His followers a good reason for not worrying or being anxious, and the reason was that they have a heavenly Father who cares about them, and knows what they need. Matthew 6:31,32.

As a young person, I had a lot of fears about a lot of things, and when I became a Christian I found that the Lord was gradually setting set me free from my fears. I noticed that whenever I found myself in a situation that provoked fear in me, if I turned to the Lord to praise Him, the fear would go. Not always immediately, but ultimately it would go. Then, while reading Psalm 34:1-8, I began to understand why.

In Psalm 34 David says, 'I sought the Lord and He heard me and delivered me from all my fears.' Interesting to note, then, that those verses are preceded by the words, 'I will extol the Lord at all times, His praise will always be on my lips'. So what is the connection between 'thanking and praising' – 'extolling God', and being delivered from fear?

David, who wrote the Psalm while fleeing for his life, had very real, strong, fighting enemies of whom he was afraid. It's a bit different for us. Many of our fears or anxieties are about non physical enemies like our bank balance, our jobs, our health, our relationships (or lack of them). We may be afraid for our children's future, or our own, and the fear can grow if we feel powerless to do anything about these things.

If we are in a dark room and turn on the light, the darkness goes in an instant. Light and darkness can't exist together. In the same way fear and faith can't exist together. Fear is the opposite of faith and so it can't thrive where there is faith. So instead of feeling bad about our very real fears, or trying to battle them ourselves, or persuade ourselves that 'it', whatever 'it' is, will never happen, we need to get ourselves filled with faith.

David says in another psalm 'The Lord is my light and my salvation- whom shall I fear? The Lord is the stronghold of my life-of whom shall I be afraid?' Psalm 27:1. Here we have yet one more truth about our relationship with God with which to agree. As we agree with God, thanking Him that He is with us and is our 'stronghold' in times of trouble we will be turning our thoughts away from the fears and towards God.

'Thanksgiving' is the door through which faith filled thoughts come into our minds to drive out and replace the fear. And, wonderfully, because it is something we can do 'at all times' (as David says in Psalm 34:1) we can always have a ready antidote to fear.

Activation . . .

Love 'fights' fear. In fact 'perfect love (the Jesus kind) drives out fear', 1 John 4:18, so today thank the Lord that He is with you in the fearful situation. Add to that thanksgiving that He cares for you, 1 Peter 5:7, that He loves and knows you, and that He will work all things together for your good, Romans 8:28, and your faith will grow and your fear will go!!!

**Those who look to Him are radiant, and their faces
are never covered with shame**, Psalm 34:5.

DAY 39 | Thanksgiving that keeps us from grumbling

Yesterday we were looking at the need to 'remember' – with thanksgiving – all that the Lord has done for us in our past. We saw that often, when God's people didn't take the time to remember and thank Him for His faithfulness, they would go astray. Today we are going to look at how they needed that attitude of thankfulness when things were getting a little boring and they started to look back with nostalgia.

In Exodus 15 1-18, we have the song that the children of Israel sang on the shores of the Red Sea, after their great deliverance from certain death. Miriam and the women danced with their tambourines. It was a great celebration. In the midst of the narrative about what had just happened, they sang, 'The Lord is my strength and my song, I will praise Him . . . I will exalt Him.' They weren't just glad to be safe, they looked back at what had just happened; remembered who had delivered them, *and they thanked Him.*

Much later on, as they journeyed on through the wilderness, their mood took a very different turn, and it was a different story altogether. In Numbers 11:4-6, we are told, 'the Israelites started wailing and said, "If only we had meat to eat! We remember the fish we ate in Egypt at no cost !!!!!!!! (Exclamations are mine) -also the cucumbers, melons, leeks, onions and garlic. But now we have lost our appetite; we never see anything but this manna."'

We know that life is a journey and, as on any journey, our lives will have their ups and downs, their highs and lows and, of course, a great deal of routine and 'ordinary' mixed in between. The children of Israel had a really big low – their time in slavery – then a dramatic 'high' when they were delivered from the Egyptians twice in quick succession. They then had forty years of 'sameness' in the wilderness. This time was not without adventure and miracles, but it also became very challenging for them, and appeared to be particularly boring for them at meal times, because of the daily menu of 'manna'!

They couldn't be grateful in the present, even though they were no longer slaves making bricks with less and less straw. They could only remember with nostalgia some of the food they had access to in the midst of all the suffering that they had experienced as slaves. They were weary of their 'present' and so to their ungrateful minds, the past looked 'rosy' and then the nostalgia led to grumbling and complaining.

How often are we full of thanks when something dramatic happens for us? Our 'short term' memory is usually quite good, however as time goes by and life becomes a little 'Ho Hum' we can forget all of God's amazing goodness to us. We can then start to look back with nostalgia at a past time in our lives. We can even forget some of the difficulties of those times as we find ourselves discontent with our 'now'.

Paul said 'I have learned the secret of being content in any and every situation, whether well fed or hungry, whether living in plenty or want.' Philippians 4:11,12. I would guess that this was because he followed his own advice to 'be thankful' in all things. 1 Thessalonians 5:18.

We can so easily be thankful when there has been a great answer to prayer, now let us add to our list of times when we need to be thankful those seasons in our life which are difficult because of their monotony. Thanksgiving for all that God has provided today will help to curb any unhealthy nostalgia and the 'grumbling and complaining' to which that leads. Giving thanks will help us to stay content and enjoying the present.

Activation ...

Is life a little 'hum drum' at the moment? Perhaps it's time to give thanks for the 'manna' you are currently receiving ... Just a thought!!

DAY 40 | Thanksgiving and staying 'full' of the Spirit

For the last thirty nine days we have been focusing on the many different ways in which being thankful keeps us both connected to, and in faith with, our wonderful Heavenly Father. This is because thanksgiving enables us to receive and enjoy the Holy Spirit's help in the midst of all the different challenges that life throws at us.

I started these daily meditations because I believe that the Lord is wanting to 'revive' us, His people. He wants to teach us how to walk through, and not be overwhelmed by, the unhelpful atmospheres in the world around us. He especially wants to prevent the enemy from silencing us – the body of Christ here on earth, at this time. A time when our testimony is so needed when many of our family, colleagues, friends and neighbours are feeling anxious and afraid.

Today, our fortieth day, I felt drawn to the verses in Ephesians 5:15-21, 'Be filled with the Spirit'. It seemed appropriate to be looking at the connection between our forty days of 'thanksgiving' and being filled with the Spirit because Jesus, after His forty days in the wilderness, came out from that time 'in the power of the Spirit' (Luke 4:14).

Jesus had come through all the temptations, and had emerged triumphant from that time, ready to minister the love of God to the world in the power of the Spirit. It was soon after this trial that He went to Nazareth, stood in the synagogue, and read the scroll saying, "The Spirit of the Lord is upon me, because He has anointed me to preach good news to the poor. He has sent me to proclaim freedom to the prisoners and recovery of sight to the blind, to release the oppressed, to proclaim the year of the Lord's favour." Luke 4:18,19.

I believe that over these last weeks, as we have embraced the choice to thank God in many different circumstances and scenarios, we have been honouring God. We have also been building our faith and reducing the time we allow doubt, unbelief and fear to live in our thoughts. In other words, by choosing to be thankful, we have had something of negativity fast.

The encouragement Paul sent to his friends in Ephesus was to make sure that they didn't get drunk, but instead were 'filled with the Spirit'. They were to 'speak to one another with psalms, hymns and spiritual songs. Sing and make music in your heart to the Lord, **always giving thanks to God the Father for everything, in the name of our Lord Jesus Christ'.**

This passage holds the key, I believe, to why we can expect to be more full of the Holy Spirit after our forty days of 'intentional thanksgiving'. The exhortation to 'be filled' is in fact a present continuous verb. It is an encouragement to be continually being filled with the Spirit. The connection is that thanksgiving and singing create an atmosphere that the Holy Spirit loves, and in which He feels welcome.

The Holy Spirit is drawn to faith and is in fact 'grieved' by other attitudes that come out of our mouths. Ephesians 4:29-32 tells us that our precious Helper and Friend the Holy Spirit is grieved by us talking in unhelpful ways that don't build up our hearers. He is also grieved by any bitterness, anger, or malice we are holding on to; but He loves a thankful heart.

Since our bodies are the temple of the Holy Spirit, 1 Corinthians 3:16, let us continue to make our hearts a welcome dwelling place for Him. Let us continue to cultivate thankfulness, and let us keep on being filled with the Holy Spirit, at all times, and in all circumstances.

Activation . . .

Thankfulness in every situation and every circumstance is a big key to staying full of the Holy Spirit, because the Spirit is a not a 'power' only, but a beautiful person and friend. So let us use 'thanksgiving' today to make Him feel very welcome in lives.

DAY 41 | Thanksgiving and staying full of the Spirit

Today I think we should take a little more time to look at Paul's encouragement to those early Christians. The encouragement to, 'Sing and make music in your hearts to the Lord, **always giving thanks** to God for everything, in the name of our Lord Jesus.' Ephesians 5:19,20. Let us look at it in the context of being **continuously** filled with the Spirit. I think that we should do this because I felt the Lord whisper to me that as we are filled with His Spirit in a continuous way, we will also find ourselves increasingly filled with His love.

It does make perfect sense of course, because the Holy Spirit is not just there to give us His help and power, though we want both of those things, He is also wanting to pour the Father's love into our hearts, (Romans 5:5) and so we circle around to the realisation that, as we thank Him and get filled up by His Spirit, so we also make a way for our hearts to be totally filled and saturated with His love.

We all know what happens to a sponge when it gets saturated. When we lift it out of the bowl of water in which it is soaking, it starts to drip everywhere, leaking the liquid with which it is soaked. This is such an exciting thought because, in like manner, as I turn my heart in thanksgiving and seek to sing and make melodies in my heart to the Lord, I will end up, as Paul prays earlier in his letter, 'filled with all the fullness of God.' Ephesians 3:1, and so even more revelation concerning the Lord's love will invade my mind, heart and spirit.

The Passion Translation of these verses catches something that we can miss when we read them in more familiar words. Verse 19 reads 'this extravagant love pours into you until you are filled to overflowing with the fullness of God.' As we sing our psalms and hymns and offer our thanks to the Lord we get to be filled to overflowing, knowing God's love for ourselves, and then we will be more likely to 'drip' God's love everywhere we go!!

Because the love of God is filling and flowing through us we will, by faith, touch other people's lives, even when we are not consciously saying, or doing, anything that one would necessarily call 'loving'. The Holy Spirit, who is such a creative member of the Godhead, can easily prompt us to do those acts of kindness; sending a gift, giving someone a smile, or sending an encouraging text. He may lead us to express our appreciation to someone, or to value someone we have previously taken for granted, because we are now seeing them through His eyes.

We may be led to give, or ask for forgiveness, to fast and pray for someone – not out of duty but out of love. When we are filled with the Spirit, and hence God's love, any number of things can happen. Life can get to be very fruitful and exciting.

So, in our thanksgiving to God today, let us allow the Holy Spirit to immerse us in the love of God, making us saturated repositories of His love, which, in turn, will 'drip' God's love to the people around us in ways we haven't yet considered.

Activation . . .

Someone recently said that what our world needs more than anything is kindness. So while we are not going to stop looking for revival, and for new birth and signs and wonders, let us give ourselves to that which we can do in the here and now. Let us fill our mouths with 'thanksgiving' and our hearts with the love of God. Then let us spread His love and kindness into our world, from the overflow of our hearts.

DAY 42 | Thanking God for His invitations

We've all had them. Those unwelcome invitations to go and test drive a car, to view a time share option, or to visit a sale room where there is some gift incentive to tempt us to part with money, or time, that we really don't have. We usually bin those invitations, or at least put them on one side to peruse at another time.

There are other invitations, to parties, or weddings. These we don't bin. They usually have an RSVP address on them, and if we are pleased to receive them, we reply saying, 'Thank you for the invitation, I will be happy to accept', expressing our intention to be there.

Today I was looking at some of the many invitations that we have from the Lord, and I believe that He is urging us not to put aside His invitations but to respond to them; to RSVP with our gratitude and thanks, because His invitations are genuine, and are they are usually inviting us to freely enjoy Him and His blessings in some way.

In Isaiah 55:1 we have one of those amazing invitations, so different to the worldly invitations coming through our letter box or email. It is for everyone who is thirsty, and even more amazing it's for those who have no money. If you fit into that group, you are invited to come and get grain, wine and milk. Symbolic things that nourish and sustain and also, I suspect, give much joy.

Sometimes we can read these wonderful words and think to ourselves 'That's great!' We can almost feel that because we have read them, and like what we have read, that is enough. We can think that we will receive what is offered by osmosis. This may in part be true because God is so gracious, and He knows our inmost thoughts. I believe however, that our friendship with God will be more enriched if we intentionally respond, and make the choice to 'come to Him' and receive.

Responding starts with our R.S.V.P. which, I would suggest, goes something like this – "Thank You God for your wonderful invitation . . . I have great pleasure in accepting!" In other word we express our delight at getting the invitation, our confidence that it is genuine and our intention, as we accept the invitation, to 'come' to Him, whatever that looks like for us. We then need to learn how to 'drink', or 'receive' what God is offering us.

In the book of Esther we have an interesting story about a king who was giving away free drinks at his banquet. It is a helpful picture, I believe, of what it is like in God's banqueting house. At King Xerxes banquet, 'wine was served in goblets of gold, each one different, and the royal wine was abundant . . . By the Kings command each guest was allowed to drink in his own way . . . the stewards were to serve each man as he wished.' Esther 1:7,8. For me this is a beautiful picture of our heavenly King's generosity, and also of the freedom He gives us to accept His invitation, and to come and drink in our own way.

Some of us come to Him and find a 'refreshing drink' as we worship, others through communion, or reading His word. Some come and enjoy the banquet through praying in tongues and others through sitting quietly, soaking in His presence with some beautiful music. For you it may be by walking in the countryside, or sitting still and viewing a beautiful part of God's creation. We all have our unique ways of receiving.

The Lord blesses us as we come to feast and drink, in our own way. The important thing is that we say, 'Thank you, I'm so grateful for the invitation!' and that we accept it by making the time and space to be with Him in our own preferred way. I believe the Lord loves it when we respond to His invitation and come to Him with great expectancy that He will bless and refresh us, pouring His 'living water' into our life and assuaging our thirst.

Activation . . .

Today accept that invitation to 'Come', and make a time and place to meet with Him, maybe in a familiar way or possibly in a way that is new for you.

DAY 43 | Another Invitation!

Today we are looking at another of heaven's wonderful invitations. This time it is given by Jesus, and it is directed to the 'weary and burdened'. It's that amazing invitation to come to Him and find 'rest', Matthew 11:28. It feels like a very good invitation for our day, because it is clearly not just speaking to the physically weary, but also to the ones who are 'soul weary', those wearied by all the cares that this world brings to us daily.

Jesus' invitation is wonderful. He effectively says, "Come and walk closely with me". The picture of 'taking His yoke' on ourselves is not, I believe, the picture of a farmer yoking up an ox to pull his heavy plough, but the invitation of a strong ox, coming along side a weaker animal, and giving an invitation to join a partnership in which the stronger does the major part of the 'lifting'.

I also see, in my minds' eye, that the yoke that Jesus puts around our neck is actually His arm across our shoulders as we walk alongside Him. The whole picture speaks to me of love, friendship, closeness and of Jesus taking the strain out of life for us. The invitation is also about 'surrendering' to Him, thereby allowing Him to set the pace and direction of our walk. So before we say yes to this particular invitation, it is important that we count the cost.

In counting the cost, we see that the phrase, 'My yoke is easy and my burden is light', is a significant part of the invitation. Jesus is saying that in our surrendering to Him, in letting Him be the leader, we shouldn't be afraid that somehow His yoke is going to be uncomfortable – like a badly fitting yoke that chaffs. His yoke, His arm around us is, I believe, firm but also 'easy'. It's a comfortable fit for us and is not at all harsh.

The reason why His yoke is 'comfortable' is, I believe, because some of our stress and weariness is caused by driveness. It is caused by all the extra 'shoulds', 'oughts' and 'have to's' in our minds, that we put on ourselves. (You may need to listen to the conversation in your head to see if I'm not right about that). If we can surrender that 'to do' list in our heads to

Jesus, for His direction, then we might find that life becomes more restful and sweet.

In addition to all the things in our heads about which we feel burdened, we can also experience weariness and the feeling of being under a heavy load, because of the worries and concerns that we have over things about which we can do very little. There can be a feeling of powerlessness over concerns around our family, our livelihood, our health, our finances etc. and these things can also be emotionally draining.

So! As we respond to this wonderful invitation, and allow Jesus to place His yoke on us, to place His arm around our shoulders, we will need to remember that Jesus' doesn't always do things the way we would like Him to, or when we would like Him to. These worries also need to be surrendered to Jesus so that they become part of the 'casting all our cares upon Him, because He cares for us.' 1 Peter 5:7.

This invitation from the Lord could indeed have been written for such a time as this. So let us say our 'Thank you' to Him, and let us respond by coming to Him and positioning ourselves under His care. I believe His pace may be different to ours, He may correct our direction a little too, but it will be a great relief to have Him carry those things that are too heavy and burdensome for us alone.

Finally, an extra and wonderful thing about being yoked to Jesus as a 'fellow ox', is that we will be close enough to enjoy fellowship with Him as we walk together through the day. We will be close enough to hear His whispers of guidance and direction, and we may also hear, if we listen closely, His joy, His laughter and His pleasure, that we have come to Him at His bidding, and accepted His wonderful invitation.

––––––––––––––––

Activation . . .

Are there any areas of your life that need to be surrendered to the Lord's care so that you can happily walk alongside Him enjoying the 'rest' and friendship of His easy, gentle yoke?

DAY 44 | Thanksgiving and Our Heavenly Father

Over the last few days we have looked at the place of thanksgiving in our relationship with the Holy Spirit and how thanksgiving helps us to stay in a place where we can be continuously filled by Him. We have also seen how thanksgiving enables us to walk with Jesus day by day, letting Him help us with our cares and burdens. Today it felt like it was the Father's turn, and I fell to thinking about Fathers day cards.

I love reading the cards my daughters write to my husband. They don't just grab a card from the rack and sign it, they carefully choose one and then add their own thanks to him for their unique experience of, and blessing from, his fathering care. In other words they make it a very personalised expression of thanks from them to him.

It is always a thrill to see what they have noticed of his love and care for them and what has mattered to them at different stages in their lives over the past years. Sometimes what they have remembered, and what has been important to them, comes as a nice surprise. The truth is that one size doesn't fit all with cards and their messages, and so it is with our experience of, and thanks to, God as our loving Heavenly Father.

There are so many beautiful songs and hymns thanking God for who He is to us, and for His goodness and faithfulness. These can really helps us to express our love to Him. Today however I felt that we should make it our own 'Fathers day' and whenever we can, throughout the day, lift our heart to Him and say 'thank you' in appreciation for things that He has done that are personal to us.

We can ask the Holy Spirit to remind us of specific things for which we can be grateful from past years. There will be so many things, and for some it will be something big like a miraculous healing or provision, even a new baby when it was thought there would be none.

For many of us however our thanksgiving will be, I guess, for the more everyday things that have mattered to us. This could be for someone He has used to help us, for guidance or wisdom when we have needed it, even that parking space when there was no time to waste getting to an appointment or, in the case of one of our friends, catching a plane after significant motorway delays!!

It's like that lovely song, 'Count your blessings, name them one by one, and it will surprise you what the Lord has done'. Well today let us not just 'count' those blessings, but let us turn our hearts in thanksgiving to Him, our good, good, Father, and surprise Him (I'm not sure that's even possible, but we can certainly delight Him) with our thanksgiving for things it might have appeared that we've taken for granted.

Activation . . .

If you are feeling creative you could spend some time making and writing a thank you card for Him, or you could write a psalm of thanksgiving, or 'sing a new song to Him' as encouraged by the psalmist in Psalm 98. In your own way why not make this a 'Thank you heavenly Father Day', as you lift your heart to Him in gratitude throughout the day.

DAY 45 | Appreciating Our Father God

Yesterday we were thanking God for all the things that He does for us, so today I felt that we really needed to look again at the biggest thing of all for which we can thank Him: that we have been bought with a price, with all the benefits and blessings that that has brought to us. Perhaps the biggest blessing of all is that we are now His beloved children, and therefore treasured members of His ever growing family.

Children throughout the Bible are considered to be a great blessing. So when we are told that we are now 'the children of God' we can see, by inference, that we have a new identity and a great inheritance. I am going to write out in full the wonderful verses from 1 John 3:2 TPT that describe this new relationship with God.

> *'Look with wonder at the depth of the Fathers' amazing love that He has lavished on us! He has called us and made us His very own beloved children. The reason the world doesn't recognize who we are is that they didn't recognize Him. Beloved, we are Gods' children right now; however it is not apparent what we will become. But we do know that when it is finally made visible, we will be just like Him, for we will see Him as He truly is'.*

That we can call Him 'Father' is in itself an amazing thing. We haven't been 'saved' to go and work 'below stairs' in God's household as a servant. We are not even just visitors allowed to come and stay if we behave well, but we are fully accepted members of the household of God, (Ephesians 2:19) with all the love, benefits and authority that being God's child confers on us.

This gets even more exciting when we read Paul's take on what happened when we were 'born again'. He writes, *'For you did not receive a spirit that makes you a slave again to fear, but you received the Spirit of sonship. And by Him we cry "Abba, Father". The Spirit Himself testifies with our spirit that we are God's children. Now if we are children then we are heirs, heirs of God and co-heirs with Christ, if indeed we share His sufferings that we may also share in His glory.* Roman 8:15-17.

If you go to Israel you will hear the children using that beautiful word 'Abba'. It's a very intimate word for Father, much more like our word 'Daddy' than the more formal 'Father' which is translated into English from the Greek word 'Pater' and used at the beginning of the Lord's prayer. It is God's Spirit within us that enables us to use that beautiful term of endearment Abba, and it speaks to us of such total acceptance by our Heavenly Father, the Lord Almighty.

Let us never lose the wonder of all this 'truth' as we muse on these things.

Activation . . .

Today thank Him with all your heart that He has brought you into His family through Christ, and that you are now safe and secure under His Fatherly care. Show Him how grateful you are, and how much you appreciate what He has done for you by allowing you to become His beloved child, His treasure.

In the words Stuart Townend penned in 1995.

> *How deep the Father's love for us, How vast beyond all measure,*
> *that He should give His only Son to make a wretch His treasure.*

Amazing!!

DAY 46 | Thanking God that He is Good

So here's a question. What if God wasn't good? What would your life look like? It's amazing isn't it how in the Western world we take it for granted that God is good? Goodness and God have come to be almost synonymous. In fact people can be surprised, even puzzled when things go bad. "How could God allow that?" we are often asked. But it wasn't, and it isn't now, always the case that other 'gods' are seen to be good.

When Jesus walked the earth, many other gods were worshipped. Even in Israel there were the temples and shrines to the Roman and Greek gods that had come with the empire. These gods were a mixed bag. Some were warlike, others fickle. Some were in complicated relationships with each other, and most of them demanded sacrifices and needed to be pacified, or bribed before they would do their adherents 'good'.

The Jews on the other hand had always had a God who was good, but sadly over the years they had covered over the goodness of God with their legalistic rituals and demands of their own creation. They had confused the simplicity of their faith that God is 'Love' and 'Goodness', with their religious rule book.

Picture the scene then as Jesus comes into the world to reveal God as Father. He heals the sick, raises the dead, sets the captives free and brings forgiveness and good news to the poor, all for free. No wonder 'the large crowd listened to Him with delight' Mark 12:37. He offered everyone a new life, and all at His expense.

He came with the news that God was good, that He loved the whole world, and that He was making a way for all who wanted to, to come and find Him without all the ritual, sacrifice and idolatry that was all around at the time. He showed the people who their Heavenly Father was and what He was like. He said 'If you have seen me you have seen the Father', John 14:8,9, and they liked what they saw.

It was Jesus that taught them that God was a good Father, a God they could talk to and ask for daily bread and protection, Matthew 6:9-13. It was Jesus who taught them that they didn't need to worry because this God knew what they needed and He cared for them, Matthew 6:25-34. He taught them that this Heavenly Father was so much better than any earthly Father, Luke 11:13, and that He would even discipline them out of love and not caprice. Hebrews 12:6-10.

It is good to recognise how blessed we are that we have a good God, to thank Him and not take His goodness for granted in the wrong way. We also need to remember that we have an enemy who subtly attacks the character of God, (being far from good himself). This is particularly so at times when we don't understand all the things that are happening in our lives, the hard and difficult things. It's then that we can slip into having our doubts and suspicions about God's intentions towards us.

We need at those times to join Basilea Schlink in her confession, "Father I do not understand you but I trust you."* We do know that He is a very good Father, perfect in fact, and sometimes we can confess and declare 'God is good' **because** we believe it, while at other times we need to declare it **until** we **do** believe it. In this way I can choose to thank Him that I am the object of His goodness every day. This is so personal and important and will change how I face and walk through each day, whatever that day may bring.

Activation ...

Give yourself today to thanking the Lord that He is a good God, and that His intentions towards you are only good – all the time. As you do that, you can bask in the sunshine of His love and goodness. You can thank Him for the truth that today, 'His goodness and mercy **will** follow me' (Psalm 23). You can thank Him in advance because He **is** good, and since He said He would follow you with that goodness and mercy all the days of your life, you can say- regardless of what type of day it is – "Today is one of **those** days", with an entirely positive meaning.

* Basilea Schlink Quotes (Author of *My All For Him*) – Goodreads

DAY 47 | Thanksgiving that we are seated with Christ

Paul starts his letter to the Ephesians with a wonderful explanation of the gospel. He writes about the amazing truths that God had revealed to him about salvation and what happens to us spiritually when we become Christians. He describes how we were spiritually dead in our sins but then made alive through God's mercy and grace. We were then raised up and seated with Christ in the heavenly realms. Ephesians 2:2-6.

So what are these 'heavenly realms', and where are they anyway? Well we know in our material world that there are things all around us that we can't actually see, but we recognise their presence. Things like the wind, microwaves, and wifi to name a few. We are comfortable and familiar with these mysterious things that we rely on, but can't see.

The heavenly realm is also around us but not seen. It's not somewhere above the clouds, but all around us, and although we can't see it with the natural eye we can be aware of the effects of that realm on our lives. When Jesus was on earth, the heavenly realm invaded the earthly on a regular basis. We see a miracle, like the water being turned to wine. John 2:11. It is also our experience that after we have been born again things change in us and for us, and we understand spiritual realities that we didn't 'see' before. The water of our humanity becomes the wine of the Spirit.

It is such a mystery, but an amazing truth to ponder, that in the Spirit we are actually seated with, or 'in' Christ in this heavenly realm. At its simplest we can explain it in human terms like this. I have a book, and I place a bookmark inside it between some of the pages of the book. If I then put that book up on a bookshelf, that bookmark will then also rest on the shelf by virtue of being 'in the book'. We have been raised from the dead state of our old sinful life and placed 'in Christ' by His Spirit, so that where Jesus is we are too, in our spirit.

So what does all this mean for us in our lives today? Well, the first thing that comes to mind is that I need to thank Him for imputing to me all the righteousness of Christ, because there is no way I would be allowed into that heavenly realm without being clothed in the righteousness of Christ Himself. We know that, as Isaiah writes of the people of His day, all our own righteousness is like 'filthy rags', (Isaiah 64:6), and that only Jesus makes us clean enough to come into that heavenly realm.

If Jesus has been raised to that place at the Fathers' right hand, and I see that I am, 'in Christ', and therefore also raised to that place, then I will have done with all accusations of unworthiness. I will have a new boldness to talk to my Heavenly Father, praying to Him in Jesus name, because my life is now 'hidden with Christ in God', Colossians 3:3. God now sees me 'in Christ', in His Beloved, as I come to Him with that faith in my heart. In this way I can now approach the throne of grace with great confidence. (Hebrews 4:16).

Today our thanksgiving is for the fact that the Lord has raised us to that place of victory in Jesus. Our thanksgiving helps to affirm us in that faith. As I thank Him for what He has done for me and where He has seated me, my faith rises, and not only will the Father be delighted that 'I've got it', but Jesus will be blessed that His sacrifice on my behalf is being fully appreciated. 'He will see the fruit of the travail of His soul and be satisfied.' (Isaiah 53:11). This, after all, was part of the 'joy set before Him', (Hebrews 12:2), that enabled Him to endure the cross.

Activation . . .

Express your gratitude today that you are 'seated with Him in the heavenly realm', and for all the implications of that revelation for your daily life. In doing this you can be part of that great company of believers bringing joy to Him today!

DAY 48 | Thanksgiving that we share His victory

We looked yesterday at the wonderful truth that when God raised Christ from the dead, we who are 'in Christ' were also raised with Him and are now seated with Him in the heavenly realm. Ephesians 2:4-6. We were thanking the Lord for the confidence we can have in the knowledge that we are completely accepted by the Father, and that He now sees us 'in Christ'.

Today we are looking at a second reason to be thankful to God for raising us up and seating us with Christ in the 'heavenly realm', and that is that it tells us that we now share in Christ's victory. We can see what this victory looks like if we look back a few verses to the end of the previous chapter of Ephesians. (It is worth remembering that this was a letter and had no chapters and verses).

These verses tell us that Jesus Himself was, 'raised from the dead and seated at the Fathers right hand in the heavenly realms, **far above all rule authority, power and dominion . . . and God placed all things under His feet and appointed Him to be head over everything for the church**, which is His body, the fullness of Him who fills everything in every way.' Ephesians 1:20-23.

The fact that Jesus is described as seated in this way indicates that His work is complete. This resonates with His cry from the cross, 'It is finished' John 19:30. He won a total victory at Calvary and now, although there is still a 'mopping up' operation to do until that victory is finally manifested at the end of the ages, God has said to Him: 'Sit at my right hand until I make your enemies a footstall for your feet' (Hebrews 1:13, Acts 2:34).

Jesus is seated, and we are seated with Him!! His work to defeat Satan is complete, and He is now 'at the right hand of God interceding for us.' Romans 8:34. He prays for us that we will be 'transformed into His likeness with ever increasing glory' 2 Corinthians 3:18. His work of intercession is now bringing us, His bride, into all the benefits of His victory.

He is praying for His body – for you and me – to be filled with everything that He is. He has already paid the price for everything on the cross, and 'His divine power has given us everything we need for life and godliness through our true knowledge of Him who called us by His own glory and goodness' 2 Peter 1:3. NASB. This is very good news and something to remember daily with a thankful heart.

We are His body on earth, and since we are raised and seated with Him in that heavenly realm, we are also in place to share that victory with Him. His plan is to fill us with all that He is, so that we can now fight our battles with Him from a place of victory. No wonder Paul could declare, despite all the hardships he went through, 'We are more than conquerors through Him who loved us.' Romans 8:37.

As we grasp these truths, we will see ourselves no longer as victims of our circumstances, but rather as 'more than conquerors' in Christ, and we can then begin to fully avail ourselves, by faith, of all the riches that are ours in Him. As we live through all the challenges of life here on earth, with our spirits raised up in Christ, we will also find ourselves being transformed from above into His likeness.

Activation . . .

As a joint heir with Christ, Romans 8:17, seated with Him in the spirit in His place of victory, you can most certainly give thanks for all that He has done for you. Your 'thanks' becomes a declaration and an affirmation of your faith, as you learn how to appropriate His victory in the challenges of your daily life.

DAY 49 | Being seated with Christ and prayer

A further thought for us today, coming out of our understanding of the truth that we are 'seated with Christ in the heavenly realm', concerns the effect that this can have on how we pray. If we are seated with Christ, and know that He has all authority and also that He is interceding for His people, then we too can pray with Him from the throne, with the authority He confers onto us as 'the royal priesthood' that we now are. 1 Peter 2:9.

When Jesus spoke with His disciples about the mystical connection they had with Him He used the picture of a vine and its branches. He spoke of the need to 'abide', or 'remain' in Him, John 15:5 and, in the course of that dialogue He gave the astonishing promise, 'the Father will give you whatever you ask in my name' John 15:16.

We all know from experience that this is not about tacking the words 'in Jesus name' on the end of our prayers. But what if 'in the name of Jesus' is more about praying as Jesus would, or as He is in fact currently praying for us and others, from His place of victory in heaven, seated at the Fathers right hand?

If we are seated with Christ, and are praying as He is praying, I am certain that the Father will indeed give us what we ask 'in His name'. In other words instead of praying, as it were, like beggars outside the castle gates, hoping for an audience with the King, we pray as children of that same King, seeing ourselves as joint heirs with Christ, and having the same access to the Father. This is because He now sees us as His beloved children 'in Christ'.

This still leaves us with a challenge. How do we know how and what Jesus is praying so that we can pray as He is praying. Well, in this respect, we have a beautiful friend and helper in the Holy Spirit who, Jesus said, will 'bring glory to me by taking what is mine and making it known to you.' John 16:14. This then is another reason to worship and give thanks as we come to pray so that we will be 'full of the Spirit' (Ephesians 5:18-20), and led by Him in our praying. (see Romans 8:26,27)

If we take a look at the Lord's prayer, with these thoughts in mind, the words 'Your Kingdom come, your will be done, on earth as it is in heaven' Matthew 6:10, take on new meaning. Even if we can't really discern what the Lord is wanting us to pray for in a particular situation, we can still pray in agreement with Him that He will do what will advance His Kingdom on the earth in that situation. Then we can confidently say, "For Yours is the Kingdom, the power and the Glory. Amen."

As we see ourselves 'seated with Christ' and as we pray from that place of victory, we can also begin to understand the words Jesus spoke to Peter after His declaration about the building of His church. He said, "whatever you bind on earth shall have been bound in heaven, and whatever you loose on earth shall have been loosed in heaven." Matthew 16:19. NAS. When we pray for something to happen on earth and it is what Jesus is praying and ordaining in heaven, then clearly it will be done.

Activation ...

Today as you pray, begin by thanking God for seating you alongside Him in His heavenly realm. Then pray from the throne with that perspective, thanking Him that He has won the victory and that you, with Him, can release that victory over situations and people as you pray in faith. Thank God with the confidence that, helped by the Holy Spirit, you are partnering with the King of Kings who has won the victory for all time.

DAY 50 | Thanksgiving for His names

We might ask the question, What's in a name? In our culture a name is just a name, something we are given soon after birth to identify who we are in our family and then in life. In some cultures a name may have an aspirational meaning for the person's character, or their future life. For others the name given may well denote a family line, but it will not in any real sense tell us who that person is in essence.

My name is Stella, it means star, but no one expects that I will in actual fact be found in the sky, shining brightly at night! When God gives himself a name however, it is different. His names tell us who He really is in essence. In the Bible we read that in different places and at different times God calls Himself by various names, and the name given was usually appropriate to the need the people, or a person, had at that time. God declares who He is by many different names, and each one conveys to us, His people, an essential aspect of who He wants to be for us.

In the Old Testament when God wanted His people to get to know who He was for them, He connected His various acts of deliverance to the name 'Jehovah', meaning 'the Lord'. We too can learn who He wants to be for us by having a look at what He called Himself at various times. To name a few we read of *Jehovah–Jireh*, 'The Lord who provides'. Genesis 22:13,14. *Jehovah-Rophe*, 'The Lord who heals'. Exodus 15:26. *Jehovah-Nissi*, 'The Lord is my banner', or 'The Lord who fights for me'. Exodus 17:15. *Jehovah-Tsidkenu*. 'The Lord our righteousness', Jeremiah 23:5,6.

There are many other names for God In the Bible like 'Wonderful Counselor, Mighty God, Everlasting Father, Prince of Peace Isaiah 9:6, *El-Shaddai*- 'the Almighty or All sufficient One', Genesis 35:11 *Emmanuel* – 'God is with us', Matthew 1:23, and of course, *Abba* Father. Romans 8:15.

We also have the names that others have given God, according to how He revealed Himself to them in their times of need. Hagar knew Him as 'the God who sees', Genesis 16:13. David, in his psalms spoke of God as his shepherd, his rock, his refuge and high tower. God doesn't just have one or two names like you and me, but each of His many names is deeply significant and important to us in our walk of faith.

Today I believe the Lord is asking us a question, *"Who do you need me to be for you today?"* as we are looking at the power of thanksgiving to release our faith in God, for Him to be for us what we need Him to be. Let us find that 'name of God' that is important for us today, and personalise it by saying, for example, 'Thank you Lord that you are my provider'. As we thank Him our faith will rise and we will see that He is who He says He is, and will do for us what His name declares.

There may not be an immediate intervention in our lives, and this I believe is because God is interested in our relationship with Him. He does not just want to 'do' things for us because we call Him by the right name, but He wants us to get to know Him better and grow closer to Him. He wants our faith to grow, like Abraham's did as he waited for his promised son for many years, whilst giving glory to God. Romans 4:20,21.

Activation . . .

As one lovely recently released song says so beautifully, 'He's in the waiting'. If you intentionally thank Him for who He is, even as you wait for Him to act on your behalf, you will grow in trust and confidence, that He is in truth your *Jehovah –Shammah* , 'The God who is there', Ezekiel 48:35.

There for you in every circumstance.

DAY 51 | Thanksgiving for His Presence

Today I have in my mind's eye a picture of a watering hole in the desert, and the first verse of Psalm 42. The psalmist likens himself to a deer longing for some water, only he is longing to find the refreshment found in meeting with God. He wants to find himself in God's presence.

These verses in the Amplified Bible and also The Passion Translation, have the psalmist as longing to 'see, or behold the face of God', which is probably because there is no word for presence in Hebrew, so the word 'face' is used when speaking of being in someone's presence. This is, for example, why Hagar, when removing herself from Abraham's household, says, 'I flee from the face of my mistress Sarah' Genesis 16:8.

In Numbers 6:24-26, God tells Aaron, through Moses, to bless the people by saying those wonderful words: "The Lord bless you and keep you, The Lord make His face to shine upon you and be gracious to you; the Lord turn His face toward you and give you His peace." It is a blessing I think that we all love to hear spoken over us.

I think there is a sense in which we would all like to find ourselves in God's presence more often. We'd like to 'see His face', but like the deer searching out a watering hole in the drought, it sometimes seems that we are looking for something that is very illusive. It can be even harder when our usual routes to our regular 'watering holes' are blocked and our regular ways of coming into God's presence are no longer available.

I believe the Lord is wanting, at this time, for us to come into a greater realisation of His immanence. He wants His people to know, at a deeper level, that He is always with them and that He is 'an ever present help' particularly in 'times of trouble' Psalm 46:1. He is our Emmanuel, the God who is with us, and so we can turn and seek His face, and know His presence whenever, and wherever, we want, without having to be in a special place or building.

The deer when approaching the watering hole has to look carefully to make sure that there are no predators around, if he is to drink peacefully. Our main predator, the devil, who 'prowls around like a roaring lion seeking someone to devour' 1 Peter 5:8, will try to make sure that we too will not be able to come freely into the Lord's presence to be refreshed by Him in a relaxed way.

In order to disturb our peace as we set aside time to 'meet with God' our enemy, who doesn't have teeth and claws, but lies and accusations, will attack. Our main defense against those lies is the truth, and as we have said in a previous meditation, thanking God for those truths rather than arguing with the devil is our most powerful defense.

Satan may try to tell you that you are not worthy to meet with God, and remind you of the mistakes you have recently made. Or he may tell you that you are not spiritual enough, and that really at least a day's fasting and prayer is required before you will encounter the Lord in any significant way.

Well, he's maybe right in some of his accusations but don't argue, instead turn away from looking at your performance and start thanking the Lord for the truth that you are clothed in His righteousness, that He loves you and is always with you. Remember that we can always enter His gates 'with thanksgiving'. {Have a look at Day 1 again and Psalm 100:4}

Activation . . .

Today as you sit quietly, take a deep breath and just say out loud if you can, 'Thank you Jesus that you are here, thank you Lord that you are with me, right now, and thank you that I can do nothing to deserve your presence but that you delight in me and that I have come aside to meet with you, to seek your face.'

Stay there a while, read some scripture, listen to some worship, have a drink and you will be refreshed, and may *"The Lord bless you and keep you, The Lord make His face to shine upon you and be gracious to you; the Lord turn His face toward you and give you His peace".*

DAY 52 | Thanksgiving and Joy

Joy is such a significant part of our faith. The Oxford dictionary defines joy as 'a vivid emotion of pleasure', and we know that God created us and Jesus redeemed us, to bring Him joy. Our faith is one that has joy at its heart, because joy is an essential part of who God is, and therefore joy fills the atmosphere of heaven. Joy, however, can sometimes be a rather elusive thing, both to define, and to experience.

We know that there was great joy and celebration, initiated by heaven, when Jesus was born and the plan of salvation, held for so long in God's heart, began to unfold on the earth. The angels spoke of 'good news of great joy' Luke 2:10, and all of heaven was celebrating. There is also great joy in heaven whenever someone turns to the Lord, and Jesus' sacrifice yields more fruit in another life saved. (Luke 15:7).

In the Old Testament, the Children of Israel experienced significant times of joy when they experienced great deliverance from their enemies. A beautiful prophetic description of that joy is written down for us in Isaiah's prophecy. 'The ransomed of the Lord will return, they will enter Zion with singing; everlasting joy will crown their heads. Gladness and joy will overtake them, and sorrow and sighing will flee away'. Isaiah 35:1-10

We know that joy is something Jesus wants us to have because He said, 'as the Father has loved me, so have I loved you. If you obey my commandments you will remain in my love . . . I have told you this so that my joy may be in you and that your joy may be complete.' John 15:11. The apostle Paul picks this up and writes about joy as an essential part of our life in Christ explaining, 'The Kingdom of God is not a matter of eating and drinking but righteousness, peace and joy in the Holy Spirit.' Romans 14:17.

It's not that God ignores our sorrows or our pain. Jesus was 'a man of sorrows and familiar with suffering' Isaiah 53:3, but He was also, we are told, anointed with the oil of joy. (Hebrews 1:9). In fact one of the things that Jesus came to do was to comfort those who mourn in Zion, to give them beauty for ashes and 'the oil of joy for mourning, the garment of praise for the spirit of heaviness; that they might be called trees of righteousness, the planting of the Lord, that He might be glorified.' Isaiah 61:3. AV.

So today I believe the Lord is calling us to a time of joy and celebration. We may not have a wedding or a birthday to celebrate. It's not a time of festival like Christmas, but celebration and joy can be ours every day, if we can learn how to 'rejoice in the Lord' in all our circumstances. So how do we celebrate and experience joy when we are in ordinary seasons of life; when we are experiencing weariness, grief and loss, anxiety, loneliness or just boredom.

We said earlier that joy can be an elusive emotion to look for, but it is one of the fruits of the Spirit, something the Holy Spirit will produce in us if we allow Him to keep filling us. We can ask the Holy Spirit, our helper and friend, to lead us into joy by showing us more of the wonders of our salvation, by making us aware of the Lord's loving help, protection and care for us over past years, and we can ask Him to highlight to us all the good things, big and small, in our lives that we are taking for granted.

As we thank Him for these things we will start on the journey of rejoicing in the Lord, which will lead us on to being 'filled with an inexpressible and glorious joy.' 1 Peter 1:8 (Written to Christians experiencing great trials).

Activation . . .

David, at a time of great testing says to the Lord, 'You have made known to me the path of life; you will fill me with joy in your presence.' Psalm 16:11. So bless and thank the Lord, for everything the Holy Spirit brings to mind, and 'may the God of hope fill you with all joy and peace as you trust Him, so that you overflow with hope by the power of the Holy Spirit.' Romans 15:13.

DAY 53 | Thanksgiving that we have an 'unchangeable' God

It is a wonderful truth that our God is an 'unchanging' God. We are told that 'Every good and perfect gift is from above, coming down from the Father of heavenly lights, **who does not change like shifting shadows.'** James 1:17. When something is lit up by the sun, the shape of its shadow can change significantly according to how the sun is catching it. If it is a person, as they turn around, the shape of their shadow will change and prove to be an unreliable source of information about that person's size. Well God isn't like that. He is who He is, consistently and unchangeably.

The writer to the Hebrews speaks of Jesus unchanging nature both before coming to earth, while on earth, and now in heaven praying for us. 'Jesus Christ', he writes, 'is the same yesterday, today and forever'. Hebrews 13:8. This is such good news and not something that we should take for granted. It means that without fail, every morning when we wake up our wonderful God is there to meet us with new mercy and fresh love and faithfulness. (Lamentations 3:22,23).

I guess in the human arena we have all been let down by other people, at some point in our lives, and if we're honest we have been 'changeable', in our turn, towards others. Our human changeableness can range from being fickle, to saying we will do something and then not doing it, right through to letting someone down significantly by deception or betrayal.

The human condition is not one of consistency, and so sometimes when things don't go the way we expect on our life's journey with God, we get disappointed with Him and project onto Him our human frailty. We may believe He has let us down, and we can even lose faith.

Joseph was a young man of vision. He'd had a dream, and in those days the belief that God spoke through dreams was strong, which is probably why his family were so angry with him. Joseph believed that the dream was God telling him of his future leadership, even over his family, and he probably presumed that this would take place in the near future, within a few years.

It may have seemed to Joseph that God had changed His mind and let him down badly as he found himself, first of all kidnapped, then left to die, sold as a slave, accused of attempted rape, thrown in prison and then disappointed by a 'friend' in whom he had put his hope. We can read the whole story in Genesis Chapters 37-47.

Many years later, at the end of the story, and when the dream has been fulfilled, and Joseph is now second only to Pharaoh in the land of Egypt, Joseph's brothers come to him. They are fearful that Joseph will take his moment and get his revenge because their father Jacob has died.

Joseph's answer stands as an encouragement to us all, for all time. He says "Don't be afraid ... You intended to harm me but God intended it for good to accomplish what is now being done, the saving of many lives. So then, don't be afraid. I will provide for you and your children." Genesis 50:15-21.

It would appear that, through everything, Joseph realised that the one person in His life who had not betrayed Him or let him down was God. So remember today that God is your unchanging Father, and, if there are some doubts and questions in your mind about God's faithfulness, or it feels as if God has let you down in some way, remember Joseph, and believe that your unchanging God is working out His plans and purposes, even though you don't understand Him.

Activation ...

Spend time today thanking God for His 'unchangeablness', and declare with the psalmist 'The Lord will fulfill His purpose for me; your love O Lord endures forever –' Psalm 138:8.

DAY 54 | Thankfulness when we don't understand

Yesterday we were considering how God remained unchanging in His intention towards Joseph and in the purpose He had for Joseph's life. Joseph went through all kinds of trials, not just because his brothers were jealous and mean to him, but because God knew that if he was to fulfill the role that God had planned for him on the world stage, he needed to grow up and mature in many, many ways.

We don't know how Joseph processed all the ups and downs of his journey, but we do know, because we know the end of the story, that we have a faithful and an unchangeable God. Joseph's story, as we said yesterday, is a wonderful encouragement for us when we feel as if God has changed His mind about us, or about a promise He has given us in the past.

As we said yesterday Joseph was let down successively by family, employers and friends across the whole spectrum of betrayal, during his time of slavery and imprisonment. There must have been so many opportunities to be angry, hurt, resentful, and vengeful. He may have felt great grief, self pity and despair. And dare I say it? Had he lived in the 21st century, he could easily have taken on a victim spirit or, at the very least, a spirit of rejection.

Had Jeremiah been around during those long years, he may have joined him in saying, 'I remember my affliction and my wandering, the bitterness and the gall. I well remember them, and my soul is cast down within me, yet this I call to mind and therefore I have hope; Because of the Lord's great love we are not consumed, for His compassions never fail, they are new every morning; great is thy faithfulness. I say to myself, "the Lord is my portion; therefore I will wait for Him".' Lamentations 3:19-24.

The truth is that Joseph prospered where ever he went; first in Potiphar's house, and then in the prison, where he was given leadership and responsibility. (Genesis 39:1-23). The Lord was training and preparing Him for future greatness. It wasn't just in the skills of leadership and administration in which he was trained however, God was interested in his character, and at the end of it all and through all his trials, Joseph had become like his God, compassionate, merciful, faithful, wise and astute.

How wonderful! In spite of how it looked humanly speaking, God had been faithful to his word. The difficulties were not because God had changed His mind about Joseph, but because He was getting this cocky, spoilt young man to a place of maturity; a place where he could carry responsibility in a way that honoured God.

Yesterday we noted that Joseph didn't just grudgingly forgive his brothers for all that they had put him through. He could in fact have let them stew a bit longer before letting them know that he had forgiven them, but no, Joseph chose to bless them. He promised he would look after them, 'And he reassured them and spoke kindly to them.' Genesis 50:21. It definitely sounds like Joseph had become more like his God.

If you are ever tempted to feel that God has let you down, or changed His mind about you, remember He is not just interested in what you do, but also how you do it, and who you are becoming. He has set His mind on conforming you to the image of His Son, by working all things for your good, (Romans 8:28,29) and He is never going to change His mind about that.

He is not just interested in developing our skills, but is wanting to help us to refuse to partner with bitterness, self pity, or despair. We may have a battle with this (as I suspect Joseph did) but to choose to bless those who have caused us harm, in any way, is a truly Christ like quality. (Matthew 5:43-48).

Activation . . .

Today thank God for any circumstances that have been hard to understand, and choose to thank God for, and release blessing towards those who seem to have hindered, or harmed you, on your journey through life.

DAY 55 | Thanksgiving that takes us deeper

FOMO or 'Fear Of Missing Out' is not a new phenomenon. In today's world however, that fear is increased by the social media that enables us all to view and compare the lives of other people with our own. We can often feel that we are missing out on the excitement, or adventure that we see in the lives of other people, even in the lives of other Christians.

We can be afraid of missing out on all sorts of things and it will be different things for each one of us. For us however, God's own children, it is important that we have **no fear that we will miss out on all that He has for us.** The truth is, we have an infinite God, and there is always more of whatever we need.

God wants us, His children, to know that His love, His forgiveness, His wisdom, His provision, all flows from His heart of abundance. There is never any shortage in God, not even of His plans and purposes for us when we feel we might have blown it. It's a staggering truth that when I wake up in the morning, all that I need from God, for the day ahead, is available. There is never an empty shelf, or a 'sold out' sign in heaven.

The prophet Ezekiel had an incredible vision of water flowing from the temple. The water flows and becomes a river flowing out to the east. It flows into the sea (the Dead Sea) where the waters are healed and become alive again with fish. In fact he saw that everything was alive where the river flowed. On the banks trees grew fruit every month producing food, and there was healing in the leaves of the trees. (Ezekiel 47:1-12)

As his vision starts Ezekiel is encouraged to follow his guide into the river. As he follows the water gets deeper and deeper. He is first of all ankle deep, then knee deep, and then the water reaches his hips until finally he is unable to walk and has to swim.

The picture is repeated in Revelation 22:1,2; here the river is explicitly called the 'water of life' flowing from the throne of God and the Lamb. It is a beautiful picture of the life that God pours out over us, because of Jesus. It's a river to drink from, and swim in. It's the flow of Life bought for us on the cross by Jesus, and it brings healing and fruitfulness into our lives.

This is, I believe, a wonderful picture of the abundance of the Life of God that is available to us His people. Far from us missing out, these visions speak, not just of abundance, but of an invitation to keep going 'deeper' with Him, and to know that there is always more about His amazing love to discover.

I guess for Ezekiel wading in that river, ever deeper, would have needed some determination, pushing against water takes deliberate effort. In the same way, it is also hard sometimes to venture further into God's love, because we may have to push through our negative thoughts and feelings that would serve to slow us down. Thoughts like, 'I can't ask God to forgive me for that again'. Or 'God must be so tired of me keep asking for help with this problem, I should have more faith, or just try harder'.

Pushing through those negatives and going deeper into the love of God is so much easier if we have hearts of gratitude and thanksgiving. If we can thank the Lord for what we do know of His unfathomable love, and faithfulness, we will position ourselves to receive more. A grateful heart, mind and spirit will receive His love so much more readily, and so our thanksgiving will take us ever deeper into His love.

Activation . . .

Meditate today on this wonderful paraphrase of Ephesians 3:17-19.

And I ask Him that with both feet planted firmly on love, you'll be able to take in with all Christians the extravagant dimension of Christ's love. Reach out and experience the breadth! Test its length. Plumb the depths! Rise to the heights, Live full lives, full in the fullness of God'. The Message.

There really is no end to His love and life flowing towards us.

DAY 56 | Thanking God for His graciousness with us

Aren't you glad God isn't a perfectionist? Well I certainly am. When I was a young Christian, there was much emphasis on 'walking in the Spirit'. It was how we described walking with the Lord, responding to His leading and promptings 'in the moment'. It was all very exciting, discovering that all sorts of things could happen as we responded to the Holy Spirit. For me however it led to a considerable amount of tension.

I read in Psalm 18:30, 'As for God His way is perfect' which I interpreted to mean there is a 'right' thing to be doing and a 'right' place to be at any moment. As a consequence 'walking with the Lord' felt like being on a tightrope and I feared that I might fall off at any moment. Not very restful, and definitely not 'the unforced rhythms of Grace' that Jesus talked about in Matthew 11:28 (from The Message).

If the Lord's way was perfect, mine most definitely was not, and that caused a lot of tension as I tried to 'get it all perfectly right'. Then I read, and reread, the next two verses in Psalm 18. 'For who is God besides the Lord? And who is the Rock except our God? **It is God who arms me with strength and makes my way perfect'**. The psalmist continues, 'You give me your shield of victory, and your right hand sustains me; you stoop down to make me great. **You broaden the path beneath me (no more tight rope for me!!) so that my ankles do not turn over.'**

I just love those verses. To know that while our God is perfect, He is not a perfectionist!! He is always there helping and strengthening me and 'covering' my shortcomings with His grace. He actually makes my way perfect by forgiving my shortcomings and overruling my mistakes with His love and grace. I just can't imagine how many times the Lord has 'covered' for me, but I am so, so grateful that He does.

A perfectionist is defined in the Oxford English dictionary as 'one who aims at perfection in his work' or 'one who holds that religious, or moral perfection must be attained'. Sadly although moral perfection is not highly regarded in our society, we still live in a perfectionist culture. Today it is more about our lives, our looks and our homes. The photo shopping and airbrushing of the pictures and images all around us can make us look for perfection in so many things, from our looks and our homes, our friendships and our church. We demand zero defects in so many areas of life, and we can easily look for perfection in ourselves and others with whom we live and work. We see perfectionism in every area of life, but we mustn't project that onto our God.

In the Bible there are several Greek words for our English word 'perfect' and it's important for us to know that. So for example in Matthew 5:48 where Jesus has been talking about loving our enemies, He says, 'Be perfect therefore as our heavenly Father is perfect'. Impossible? Yes, perhaps, but the word telios actually means to be complete, or matured. God wants us to be complete – like Him in our dealings with others.

The Greek words for 'perfect' all have a sense of completion, ending, bringing to maturity. Something that is perfected. They are very nuanced words not binary. That is to say they are not about right or wrong but about growing and maturing. Hence in 2 Timothy 3:17, in the AV it says, 'That the man of God may be perfect, thoroughly furnished unto all good works.' while the NIV reads 'So the man of God may be equipped for every good work'.

Activation . . .

Our God is not a perfectionist but He is 'perfecting' you. He is working to make you mature you, (Romans 8:29) and more like Jesus. So today thank God that He is on your side. He is not assessing you for how perfectly you live, but is with you helping you to grow in your walk with Him. Thank Him also for others, and allow Him to work in you that same graciousness towards others. Let there be no 'perfectionism' amongst us all, only 'compassion, kindness, humility, gentleness and patience.' Colossians 3:12, as we learn to treat each other as the Lord treats us.

DAY 57 | Thank the Lord that He is working to 'perfect' you

In yesterday's meditation we were looking at the wonderful truth that although the Lord is not perfectionist with us, He is working to 'perfect', or 'fulfill' His purpose for our lives, because He loves us. (Psalm 138:8). In addition to blessing us with good things in so many ways, the Lord also uses difficulties and problems to 'work' this perfecting process in our lives.

While we can often see the 'good' things that happen to us as blessings, and problems as a sign that we have made a mistake, or that God has left us for a season, God sees those same problems as opportunities to pour out more blessing on us, but in different ways than when life is all good and plain sailing. So today we have some alliteration for you (courtesy of Graham Cooke) that will remind you of God's intention towards you whenever you have a problem, especially one that's hard to handle.

Following all the 'Ps' we can remember that for every **problem** there will always be an appropriate **promise** for us that will help us to find the **provision** of God for that situation. I would like to add to those 'Ps' two more in the light of what we shared yesterday. They are that the **promise** and **provision** will lead to our **progress,** and move us closer to being **'perfected'** in our faith as the Lord works these things for good in our lives. (Romans 8:28).

I guess this is another way of looking at James 1:2-6, and a reason why we can be thankful for our **problems**!!!! It is certainly an easy way to help me to remember that the Lord is with me and looking to bless me as I face all kinds of challenging situations. It means that when I have a **problem**, I can genuinely start my conversation with the Lord with thanksgiving, as I look in His word for His **promises** and His **provision**.

If we don't understand His good intention towards us we could find ourselves starting our conversation with the Lord with another 'P', and **plead** with Him to help us, and of course He will. We can **plead** with Him saying 'Please help me Lord, please Help me' but we may still feel unsure about whether or not the help will come and, if we are honest, a bit unsure about whether or not God has heard us.

Let me illustrate what I mean by a little anecdote from a family holiday in France. We are travelling to our holiday home. This was before the days when Macdonalds and fast food entered the French scene. We have some hungry children in the back of the car, and no eating places in sight. One daughter begins to ask for a food stop, clearly she is feeling hungry and so grumpy and discouraged and a little cross that we haven't planned this properly and found somewhere to stop and eat.

"Please can we stop" she says, persistently and with the implication that we are being mean not to. Another daughter chirps up in an excited voice, bouncing up and down, "We're going to stop, we're going to stop, and we're going to get some chips". Our response to the one was, "Please stop complaining, we are doing our best to find a stop", and to the other it was "Yes of course, as soon as we find somewhere".

Well, of course both daughters were eventually fed, but one, I'm guessing, enjoyed the next half hour of the ride far more than the other. She had faith in us, in what we promised, and was able to wait with eager anticipation. The other probably found that half hour hard, worrying if we were taking her 'needs' seriously enough, and if there ever would be any food!

Our God is a good, good Father. He makes us **promises** that He will keep. So next time you have a **problem**, ask the Holy Spirit to remind you of the **promise** you need, then let your faith and excitement grow as you thank Him in advance for the **provision** that He is sending. Remember that as He **provides** for you, He will also be '**perfecting**' your faith.

Activation . . .

Try thanking Him in your times of need, and look to see what promise He has made and what provision is coming.

It may surprise you!

DAY 58 | Thank God for His work in your life

As we continue to think about the fact that God is 'perfecting us', or making us mature and complete, we need to have a look at 2 Corinthians 4:7. It's the part in Paul's letter where, having described himself as God's servant, and someone who has seen 'the light of the knowledge of the glory of God in the face of Jesus Christ', he then refers to himself, and his fellow workers as clay pots, (a very common sight in those days). He writes 'we have this treasure in **jars of clay**, to show that this all-surpassing power is from God and not from us'.

Other translations go for **'earthen vessels'**, **'vessels of earth'**, and **'common clay jars'**. I rather like common clay jars, or pots, because earthenware in our culture can be quite expensive and desirable, but Paul is making a clear point here that, naturally speaking, there is nothing special about him or us, we are just ordinary people. The kind of 'pots' that are used every day.

This gives us even more evidence that the Lord is not 'perfectionist' with us, but this God who, the Old Testament tells us, won't share His glory with another, (Isaiah 42:8), actually comes, and because of what Jesus has done, lives in the likes of you and me; 'common clay pots'. He doesn't even wait until we've reached a certain minimum standard. Jesus actually said when praying to the Father for His, far from perfect, disciples "I have given them the glory that you gave me" John 17:22.

We may want to smarten up the clay pot, even try to become a gold, or silver one, but it's important that we don't believe that we can't be used by Him if we aren't yet perfect like Jesus. If we do we may be in danger of putting on a religious façade, not realising that it is more about Him, the treasure we are carrying, than the common clay pot He has chosen to inhabit.

We live in a culture of celebrity, and this can spill over into the church, but this is not the case in the Kingdom. God is not perfecting us to be super stars, or celebrities in His family. The truth is that God sees us all as special.

We are His beloved sons and daughters. We are all a work in progress, so don't focus on the pot reconstruction, but let the Lord fashion you into the kind of 'pot' He wants you to be. Let the potter do His work, agreeing with Isaiah when he wrote, 'Yet you O Lord, you are our Father. We are the clay, you are the Potter; we are all the work of your hand.' Isaiah 64:8.

The call of God on our lives is to live in an ordinary way, but carrying the treasure of God and letting it spill over wherever we go. You see no one else has your exact circle of friends, your colleagues, neighbours, family. Only you touch those lives in your unique way. So the Lord is perfecting us, not to become Christian superstars, but to carry and represent Him **in the best way we can in our everyday lives**.

Sometimes the faults and failings, which haven't yet been dealt with by the Lord, can cause us to be self critical or critical of others for their unrefined 'stuff'. This criticism doesn't always help us, or others, to 'change'. It is so much better if instead we can keep our focus on staying filled to overflowing with the treasure He has placed within, by thanking Him and inviting him to fill us more and more, then His glory, the glory that we are in fact carrying will become more and more evident.

I love the line in Dave Bilbrough's song 'An army of ordinary people'. That's who Jesus is calling us to be. An army of ordinary people filled with Him. We have to recognise that our journey is not about self improvement but about being filled and reflecting His glory. Our transformation comes as we look at Jesus and find ourselves transformed little by little into His likeness with ever increasing glory. (2 Corinthians 3:18). These verses tell us that we are changed just one degree at a time as we look at Him in worship, read about Him in the Bible, respond to Him in our lives and, yes, **give thanks to Him** for all that the Holy Spirit is doing in us.

Activation . . .

Next time you feel self critical, or critical or another, try thanking God for all that He has done and is doing in you, and in others. Then thank Him that 'common clay pot' that you (and they) are, there is amazing treasure within.

DAY 59 | Thanksgiving that Grows My Faith

During the past two months we have been realising that as we focus our thoughts on God's faithfulness our faith grows. As we feed our minds, our hearts and our spirits on God's **faithfulness**, we can be **full of faith** for the challenges facing us. Moreover feelings of panic, or of being overwhelmed by a situation, subside if we can look back and thank God for His faithfulness in past situations. By doing this we are in fact drawing on our own history with God for encouragement, just as David did when he faced Goliath.

Today I believe the Lord wants us to learn how to use thanksgiving to build up our faith by drawing also on the testimony of others. Testimony that shows us how the Lord could work in the same, or similar ways, for us. When we hear the testimony of friends and fellow church members we can be enormously encouraged but also, if we're honest, it can be a bit tricky to handle because, while we love to hear of what the Lord has done for those that we know, the enemy can also use the testimony of others to discourage us.

We always have a choice how we hear and receive testimony. Sometimes it is easy to be excited and encouraged by the things that the Lord has done for someone we know, especially if we have been praying for them, but what if the Lord has done something, or provides for someone, and it's the very thing that we have been wanting and waiting and praying for in our life, and yet it just hasn't happened?

Sometimes when we hear what God has done for someone else we have to guard our heart from jealousy; "Why them and not me? or maybe from feeling a bit left out, passed over by God, and left wondering, "What have I done wrong", or "Why has God blessed them and not me". Thoughts something like, "I'm clearly not as important", can go through our mind and, unchallenged, these thoughts can lock us into unbelief, as we take up the position of "That's never going to happen for me!"

I heard a lovely suggestion a while back that can get us past those thoughts and feelings, and it is simply this. If in your family, you buy an ice cream, or something nice for one child, how long before the other children are hanging on your arm saying, "Me too please". So how about when you hear a testimony that triggers something in you, you tug on your heavenly Father's sleeve and say "Me too please". In other words you take their testimony and you give thanks to God for what He has done for them – that stops the jealous or negative thoughts crashing in – and you say in your own way, "Me too please Father".

Now of course we know that sometimes any good Dad will not give the same to the second child as the first, however nicely they ask. For example He may not want to buy his six year old the same smart phone he has bought the sixteen year old. In the same way we know that our heavenly Father will be wise with us in what He grants us in response to our prayers, but if we can keep that attitude of thanksgiving it will stop us from having any kind of 'spiritual sulk'.

The Holy Spirit will remind us that, 'He who did not spare His own Son, will He not, along with Him, graciously give us all things?' Romans 8:32, and also that He is a very good Father. Our thanksgiving and praise to God for the way He has blessed another will help us to stay focused on His 'faithfulness', and help us to be 'full of faith' and expectancy for what He will do for us in a way appropriate to our need and maturity.

Activation . . .

In Revelation 19:10 we are told that 'the testimony of Jesus is the spirit of prophesy'. So when you hear a testimony, receive it with joy and thanksgiving, and thereby release a blessing over yourself, making yourself ready to receive your next miracle.

Likewise when you get blessed by something good, testify to others about what the Lord has done (in a way that honours God and not you) and release a blessing over them, that they may rise up in their faith and experience more of the Lord's goodness for themselves.

DAY 60 | Thanksgiving, growing in faith and silencing the devil

We have now been pursuing our theme of thanksgiving for two months, and it is becoming clearer and clearer that as we respond, in all the various situations of life with thanksgiving, we are in fact choosing to respond at all times with faith in our hearts. As we thank God for the opportunities that come every day to trust Him and to know Him in all the different circumstance that life throws up for us, we are in truth cooperating with the Holy Spirit, our 'alongside helper'.

Our thanksgiving opens us up to receive the infilling of the Holy Spirit. The Holy Spirit then enables us to receive the love of God, to understand His ways, to appropriate His promises and to walk with Him in faith and confidence. Thanksgiving opens the way for God to be to us all that He promises to be in and for us, and to let Him 'always lead us in triumphal procession in Christ and through us spread everywhere the fragrance of the knowledge of Him'. 2 Corinthians 2:14. Through setting our hearts to give Him thanks we are getting to see God's perspective on what is happening in our lives, and we are also expressing and growing our faith in who He wants to be for us in those situations.

This is a journey of growing in faith, and I hope you are enjoying it. I believe the Lord wants us to know today that three big things are happening on this journey of thanksgiving. Firstly we are blessing Him and His face is shining on us because He is enjoying this journey with us. Secondly we are growing in our faith in who He is for us and who He is within us and thirdly, something we might not have quite realised, we are robbing the enemy of any free parking in our minds. In fact we are giving him a headache in the sense that we are causing him a problem as to how he can get to us!

The devil can't stand us believing God, or thanking Him and honouring Him with our praise, but then there is the additional problem for him because, as we fill our minds and hearts with gratitude, we will also be shutting out the lies and half truths – the doubts and fears – with which he tries to feed us.

If we don't listen to him, and don't receive his lies he has no power over us. This is because his power depends on us entertaining, believing, and then even acting on his lies.

Our thanksgiving raises our faith in the Lord and drowns out the enemy. I think that deserves a spiritual 'high five'. So today let us recommit ourselves to pursuing 'thanksgiving' as our lifestyle and see what encouragements the Lord has for us over the next few months, and what He will do in our lives as we travel this road with Him.

Activation . . .

Today you could list here any changes in yourself that you have observed over the last two months, remembering that this is just the beginning!

DAY 61 | Thanking God for the breath of life

When Moses asked God what name he should give to the Israelites should they ask the question, "Who has sent you?", the name that God gave Himself was YHWH (which we now write as YAHWEH). These four consonants are known as the aspirated or breath consonants because the sound they make is like someone breathing out.

I think it is fascinating that the main sign of life for us as human beings is that we are breathing. Our respiratory system is a creation of pure genius. Breathing takes oxygen to our lungs and then into our cardiovascular system, and then our blood does this amazing thing of travelling around our body distributing good things and removing the bad. But it all starts with breath, and until that new born takes its first breath there is no sustainable life.

In Genesis 2 when God had created the world with animals and plants He then created humankind, and, in verse 7, we are told that He did something of great significance. He formed man from the dust of the earth and then 'breathed into his nostrils the breath of life and man became a living being'. The bible doesn't tell us that God breathed into all the animals, and though He might have done so, I think that somehow the Holy Spirit, by just leading the writer to tell us that this was how Adam came alive, is indicating that there is something very different about humankind.

I believe the bible is telling us that man may have been made from earthly elements but the breath that the Lord breathed into Him was not just nitrogen, oxygen and carbon dioxide, not just air, but the Lord breathed into Him of His own nature and Adam became a living human being and also a spiritual being. One of the things that Elihu got right in his conversation with Job was his statement that 'The Spirit of God has made me; the breath of the Almighty gives me life.' Job 33:4.

We are not just human beings with a soul, with which we can think and feel and make choices but we are also spiritual beings capable of connecting with God Himself. The fact is that you and I are living spirits, housed in a body which will one day die and decay, while our spirit, the life that God has breathed into us, will live on.

We often, understandably, give much attention to our body, to our mind and emotions, caring for them and keeping them fit and healthy, which is absolutely the right thing to do, we are after all the temple of the Holy Spirit, 1 Corinthians 6:19; but somehow we can neglect to give the same care and attention to looking after our spirits.

At the end of his letter, Paul blessed the Thessalonian church with the words 'May God Himself, the God of peace, sanctify you through and through. May your whole spirit, soul and body be kept blameless at the coming of our Lord Jesus Christ.' 1 Thessalonians 5:23,24.

One very good way to keep our spirit, as well as our body and soul 'blameless' is to stay in a spirit of gratitude and thankfulness whatever comes at us in life. Phyically we know that, providing we have no lung disease, we will breathe in and out effortlessly and naturally and that that breath will sustain our life. In the same way we need to be constantly effortlessly thankful as we go through the day, so that whatever comes at us, we remain in a healthy place spiritually. As we practice and grow in this we will stay vibrant in our spirit and in close connection with God.

Let us thank God today for every breath that we take, for the amazing design and working of our lungs. And let us also breathe into our spiritual lungs the 'air' of heaven. Let us breathe in the 'life of God' throughout the day by thanking Him for His unfailing presence – with us in all circumstances – and for all the goodness that He brings into our lives.

Activation . . .

Holy Spirit today I ask you to create in me a 'heart of thanksgiving' so that I may effortlessly day by day, moment by moment, increasingly breathe in the 'air' of heaven. Amen.

DAY 62 | Thanksgiving that grows my spirit

In their book *Blessing your spirit** Sylvia Gunter and Arthur Burk introduce us to the idea that we can 'grow' our spirit; that our spirit is not given to us like one of our physical attributes such as our height, or the colour of our eyes, which is in our genetic code. The spirit within us, that came alive to Him when we were born again, is something we can grow and develop even as we can develop our minds and our physical abilities.

Throughout the New Testament there is encouragement, and even expectation, that we will be growing in maturity in Christ, and these two authors have reminded us, in a fresh way, how we can be instrumental in growing or strengthening our spirits as we cooperate with the Holy Spirit's work in our lives.

They point out that for some of us our minds and emotions are far stronger, far more developed than our spirits, and so it can be hard for us to hear the Lord or to know His love and His leading in our lives. If we are to be 'led by the spirit' we all need to allow the Holy Spirit to keep filling us, Ephesians 5:18,19, and we also need to do all we can to 'build up' or 'grow' our own spirit.

In the New Testament we read of four distinct ways in which we can 'grow' our spirit. Firstly, from Ephesians 4:9-13, we see that we can grow spiritually through the ministry of gifted leaders in the church. The apostles, prophets, evangelists, pastors and teachers. Their ministry is to build us up until we all attain to the 'whole measure of the fullness of Christ'. These ministries the Lord calls and equips as 'gifts' to His body, and we have probably all been blessed by such ministries. If we can receive their input as a gift from God, with thanksgiving (as well as discernment), we will grow and mature under their care. Honouring them in this way with a thankful heart, Jesus said, positions us to gain the reward. (See Matthew 10:41).

Secondly in Ephesians 4:15,16 Paul tells us that our spiritual growth comes as we build each other up in love, by speaking truth to each other. Not pointing out faults, as some have used this verse, but reminding each other of truths which will feed our spirits and cause us to mature in our faith.

The third way in which we, as individual believers, are encouraged to build ourselves up is through feeding on God's word to us. Paul spoke to the elders from Ephesus and encouraged them with the words 'Now I commit you to God and the word of His grace, which can build you up and give you an inheritance among all those who are sanctified.' Acts 20:32. God's word is now written down for us in both Old and New Testaments. As we read it, not just for information, but with a thankful heart, it will be working in us the transformation we long for.

Finally Paul encouraged the Christians in Corinth to 'edify' themselves, build themselves up by using the gift of tongues, their spiritual language, and yet another gift from God, 1 Corinthians 14:4. Jude also exhorted his friends, in his letter, with the words 'build yourselves up in your most holy faith and pray in the Holy Spirit.' Jude, verse 20.

So we have four wonderful gifts from God with which we can build ourselves up and grow our spirits to become strong, mature and more Christ like. We have those in our lives with gifting to help us grow, we have our fellow believers in the body, we have God's word, and we have the indwelling spirit praying from deep within with our spirit.

Activation . . .

Today be intentional to receive these gifts with thanksgiving, with the gratitude that they warrant. You will then find that they will bear maximum fruit in your life as you seek to follow the Lord. All four will help to 'grow' your spirit and make you more like Jesus day by day.

Blessing Your Spirit, Sylvia Gunter and Arthur Burk. Published by The Father's Business 2005.

DAY 63 | Thanksgiving that keeps us 'full of faith'

We have considered in recent days how keeping ourselves **full of faith** often comes from feasting our hearts on God's **faithfulness**. The illustration that comes to mind is of a ball, which represents the challenge before us, and the sun which represents God. If we hold the ball, small as it is, up in front of our eyes, we can completely block the sun from our view.

This can be what happens if we hold our problem up to the Lord, and try to see past it in order to pray and have faith that He is big enough, or even willing to help us. The problem can fill our view and block God out. In order to stay **full of faith** in the challenges that we face, we need to put the ball – our problem – down, and turn our gaze to the sun – our God – to see how big, and powerful, and beautiful He is in comparison.

If we can draw on our own history with Him and also rejoice in all that we see He has done for others, it will help us to keep our gaze on God's **faithfulness** and not on the latest 'giant' to come across the horizon and into our world. We will stay **full of faith** in the face of those fresh challenges if we can keep our eyes on Him as we thank Him and recall past deliverances, like John Newton who, in his hymn, wrote the wonderful line 'His love in time past forbids me to think He'll leave me at last in trouble to sink'.

Sometimes, when we are feeling low or overwhelmed, we can be a bit like the rabbit in the headlights and our mind just goes blank when we try to recall past miracles, or we can even be tempted to dismiss them as coincidence. So today we want to turn our attention to all the stories in the Bible which speak of the Lord's faithfulness, written down for our encouragement.

It always amazes me how, although the bible and particularly the Old Testament was written thousands of years ago, and although life has changed beyond all recognition, politically, economically, technically and socially, from those days, those stories can nevertheless be so relevant to my life today as they reveal the unchanging character of the Lord.

Reading of His willingness to deliver His people from all sorts difficulties causes our faith to grow for our own situations, and as we read the written word, we can thank God for what is revealed to us of His character. Furthermore the Holy Spirit will highlight relevant aspects of the narrative to us of God's love and His power, causing our faith to grow.

We also have the biographies and histories of Christians from all over the world, from past centuries and from recent times and we can get inspired by these stories too. Sometimes we may feel very ordinary in comparison, but if we read these books, not comparing ourselves, but keeping our eyes on how the Lord has worked in their lives, if we can stay thankful for their example and for the testimony of the great things God has done for them, then we will be encouraged.

Our thanksgiving pulls those testimonies right into our present, and it also destroys any negative unbelief. It is like removing the small ball that represents our problem away from our eyes, so that we can see 'the sun' our Lord Jesus, and all that He wants to be for us.

So next time, or even right now, if you need faith for a situation, let the Holy Spirit remind you of a comparable situation from the bible, or of a testimony from someone else's life and just say to the Lord, "Thank you for reminding me, I'll have some of that in my own life please".

Activation . . .

I believe this is part of the invitation to 'taste and see that the Lord is good' Psalm 34:8. Put this to the test and see what will happen. It could make life very exciting from now on!

DAY 64 | Thanksgiving for our impossibilities

Continuing with our theme of keeping ourselves 'full of faith', today we are going to think about thanking the Lord for our 'impossibilities'. We can read about so many amazing miracles in the bible. These miracles, it seems to me, usually happened in the face of an impossibility, and we God's people need to see the miraculous again in our 21st century technologically advanced society.

The fact is, we need to have an 'impossibility' before we can see a pure miracle. So the children of Israel saw the Red sea part, and they walked through on dry land. (Exodus 14:13-31). The servants filled the jars with water because there was no more wine, and as they served it they saw that Jesus had turned it into wine. (John 2:7-10). The woman with the issue of blood, had tried everything to get better for twelve years to no avail, and then she touches Jesus robe and she was instantly healed. (Mark 5:24-34).

So many of the miracles and healings that we read of in the Old and New Testaments, come when there is nowhere else to go, but to the Lord. In our world we can go to doctors, search the internet, and find support in all kinds of ways, practical and financial, and nearly all of these things are good, and God can and will work through them. I am thinking today however that the Lord wants us to get to know Him as the 'God of the impossible'.

One area where God has shown Himself to be the God of the impossible is 'barreness'. We read about Sarah, Rebecca, Hannah, Elizabeth and of course Mary. They were all childless for different reasons, but all received a miracle child when there wasn't the slightest possibility of them giving birth at all.

Sometimes the miracle was desperately sought, as when Samuel was born. 1 (Samuel 1:9-18). At other times it was a total surprise, as we see with Mary, (Luke 1:26-38). On several occasions it was a very delayed response to prayers prayed long before, as with Sarah (Genesis 15:1-6) and Elizabeth, (Luke 1:25).

In each of these miracles, God had purposed that it should be clear that it was His hand and His alone that had created the miracle birth, and the people involved knew that they had been drawn into the purposes of God big time. These miracles allowed God to open their eyes as to who He was and what he could do. They allowed people to know that, **'With God, nothing shall be impossible'**. Luke 1:37, AV.

The reaction I love the most is Sarah's. We are told that, on overhearing the news that she was to have a baby when she was well into her nineties, 'Sarah laughed to herself'. The Lord challenges her about this laughter, and then continues **"Is anything too hard for the Lord?** Sarah denies laughing, and gets the short response from the Lord, 'Yes you did laugh'. Genesis 18:1-12. How lovely then that when the baby is born, he is named 'Laughter' – Isaac.

In these days Jesus is preparing His bride and He wants us to be 'believing believers'. He is preparing us in the west to see those 'greater things', and He is wanting to raise our faith levels. I think He would say to us as He said to those early disciples, 'I tell you the truth if you have faith as small as a mustard seed, you can say to this mountain, "move from here to there", and it will move. **Nothing will be impossible for you'**. I believe we are on a journey of faith, the first step of which is going to be seeing our own 'impossibilities' met with a miracle.

Activation . . .

Is there something in your life that feels like an 'impossibility', something where a miraculous breakthrough is needed. Today is the day to begin to thank Him for it, whatever it is. Thank Him for this opportunity to trust Him and see Him at work, and build up your faith as Abraham did, as you 'give glory to God'. Romans 4:20.

DAY 65 | Thanksgiving that cuts through confusion

I believe that today's meditation is for those of us who find ourselves chewing over the things that perplex us rather like a dog with a bone. Now to clarify that statement there is a good way to 'chew' on things, like the cows ruminating on their food, chewing something over can be a way of getting all the nourishment out of it, so chewing things over as a meditative practice is good.

I am however thinking of the kind of 'chewing things over' that leads us deeper into confusion and frustration. It can be rather like trying to untangle a ball of string by pulling the end but just finding that you are making the knotting tighter, and you are less and less able to unravel it.

This could be chewing over some personal, or relationship dilemma, a family or work issue, a theological problem, or even something in the political world that vexes you. There are many things that can occupy our minds and tie up our thought process, and even invade our dreams.

We can often feel that if we could just think this thing through a bit more, the solution or wisdom would come. We can even seek to find answers from other people or on the web, and these can be great sources of help, but if we are finding that our confusion is growing with our deliberating, then it's time to call a halt, and time to find another way to find solutions.

It is in such situations that we can find that thanksgiving, can enable us to cut through all the knots and tangles in our thinking, and help us to clarify the issues and the solutions. This is because God is ultimately the source of all wisdom. He is also omniscient and, very importantly, extremely kind. I wonder if this is why Solomon, when he was invited to ask God for whatever he wanted when he became king, came to the decision to ask God for wisdom. (1 Kings 3:5-9)

All I know is that when I step back from chewing over a situation, and start thanking God for that very situation then, by implication, I surrender my own thoughts and feelings and begin to receive His. The tension and preoccupation generated by trying to 'think something through' goes and I can begin to listen out for 'the wisdom that comes from heaven' that is 'pure, peace loving, considerate, submissive, full of mercy and good fruit, impartial and sincere', James 3:17.

I am not saying that if you start by giving thanks for a difficult situation or relationship that is 'tying you in knots' that you will get a direct voice from heaven, but I am suggesting that your thanksgiving will free up your spirit to receive from the Lord the wisdom you need.

The wisdom you need may come directly through a scripture, a sermon, or a time of worship, but equally it may come in a variety of ways, some quite unexpected. It could come as you are taking a walk, driving your car, baking a cake, talking to someone or having a rest. You will recognise it as from the Lord, because it will look and feel right as described by James in the verses above.

There is no shortage of wisdom with God, but sometimes a little deafness on our part. There is also a different time scale with God so, a word of warning here, and that is that when we are chewing something over, we often can't let go of it **until** we have an answer or a solution. But if and when we decide to 'give thanks' for the situation, we are in fact letting it go to the Lord and He doesn't always give immediate answers. Quite often His answers, or the wisdom we need, will come at a later time, as we relax and turn our attention to other things.

Activation ...

When you next find yourself puzzling and chewing over a situation in a way that is knotting you up, use the heaven sent scissors of thanksgiving and free yourself up. Don't let thanksgiving become an alternative way of chewing things over. Let it be a faith filled turning to the Lord and a 'letting go' to Him, saying in effect "Now over to you Lord".

DAY 66 | Thanksgiving and asking for wisdom

Ask is such a funny word, such a small word and yet full of meaning and power, particularly when it comes to connection and communication, and so it's no surprise that Jesus had quite a bit to say about asking.

Jesus said "I tell you, anyone who has faith in me will do what I have been doing. He will do even greater things than these, because I am going to the Father. And I will do whatever you ASK in my name, so that the Son may bring glory to the Father. You may ASK me for anything in my name, and I will do it." John 14:12-14. "If you remain in me and my words remain in you, ASK whatever you wish and it will be given. This is to my Father's glory, that you will bear much fruit." John 15:7,8.

When I was a child there was still the perceived wisdom that it was not good manners to keep on 'asking' for things. Things should be offered, and then received with gratitude, even if the thing was not really what you wanted. There was thought to be something a bit demanding about a child, or even an adult, who was always 'asking' for something. Even today as adults we sometimes find ourselves in a position where we are reluctant to 'ask' for something in case we put someone in the position of having to say no, as sometimes that can be uncomfortable for them and for us!

Well, it would seem that our heavenly Father doesn't feel like that at all. Jesus said very clearly, "ASK and keep on asking and it shall be given to you", and also that the Father was more than willing to "give the Holy Spirit to those who "ASK, and continue to ASK Him", Luke 11:9,22. AMP. (The present imperative used here implies continuing, or repeated, action). So we have our Heavenly Father's permission, even encouragement, to come with our requests, and to be persistent with our asking.

This morning I was thinking about 'wisdom', and the fact that wisdom is another powerful weapon in our armoury. David had the Lord's wisdom when he refused to fight in Saul's armour. 1 Samuel 17:39. Joshua too, many times had wisdom from God; most notably when he led the Israelites to march around Jericho once for six days, and then seven times on the seventh day, when they were to blow their trumpets. They just couldn't have known for sure what effect their shouting would have on those walls until it happened. Joshua 6:3-5.

Wisdom is in fact something for which we are definitely encouraged to ASK, especially if we feel we are lacking it. James tells us that we should 'ASK God, who gives generously to all without finding fault, and it will be given to him. But when he ASKS, he must believe and not doubt...' James 1:5,6.

A great way to ensure that you are asking 'without doubt' for the wisdom that you need is to follow Paul's advice and 'by prayer and petition, **with thanksgiving**, present your requests to God'. Philippians 4:6.

It is so easy to ask God for wisdom and then find yourself still puzzling and fretting your way through a problem. A relaxed **'thank you'**, after you have asked, places you in a good place of readiness to receive that wisdom from above, that is 'pure; then peace loving, considerate, submissive, full of mercy and good fruit, impartial and sincere.' James 3:17. God's wisdom may also be, quite possibly, totally left field from your natural thought patterns, so be ready!

Activation...

Try ASKING for wisdom for that knotty problem that you have. ASK with thanksgiving and be ready to receive that wisdom from above. It may just surprise you!!

And, as we will be asking 'in Jesus name', it will also be 'to the Fathers glory', John 15:8.

DAY 67 | Thanksgiving that I am part of the vine

In John's Gospel chapter 15 Jesus tells His disciples that He is the vine and they are the branches. I think that sometimes the power and significance of this passage is a little overshadowed by the sneaky fear some of us have that we might prove to be a 'fruitless branch', and that we might be 'cut off'. We can then spend time wondering 'Am I OK?' and so miss the immensity of what Jesus is saying.

If you think that you might fall into that category, then let me reassure you. The fact that you are reading the Bible, or this book, would indicate a hunger to know God more and to grow in your faith. That in itself is 'fruit', and if you are looking at your life and thinking 'I don't see much fruit' perhaps you are looking for the wrong things.

Try asking yourself, 'Am I a little kinder, a little more patient these days?' or 'have I noticed that I'm not so comfortable with gossip and jealousy, as I used to be?' The point I am making is that fruit bearing is different to being perfect. We are all growing and changing, and the fact that we want to grow and do better is in itself a sign that we are 'bearing fruit'.

Returning to the wonderful truth that we nearly missed as we read these verses through, Jesus is saying that we can do nothing without Him, (verse 5) but with His life flowing through us we can bear 'much fruit' and glorify the Father. His life is the 'sap' that causes the fruit to form and grow.

John writes for us that 'On the last and greatest day of the feast, Jesus stood up and said in a loud voice (and He cried out **very** loudly), "If anyone is thirsty, let him come to me and drink, as the scripture has said streams of living water will flow from within him." By this He meant the Holy Spirit, whom those who believed in Him were later to receive.' John 7:37-39. For you and I a miracle happened when we came to Jesus. A river of life began to flow through us, and it was His very own life.

We have a couple of vines growing on our pergola. They look absolutely dead in the winter, just like dried up sticks. Unlike the signs of life that you see on some trees as their buds form in autumn ready for spring, there is not even the slightest indication of life on the vines. Every spring however a miracle happens before our eyes. First of all we see tiny green shoots, then a very small hardly noticeable pink flower. From there, when the fruit sets, we see clusters of tiny, tiny pinheads and that is all.

Then over the next five months, without any effort, those tiny little pin heads swell and grow into clusters and then bunches of grapes. The transformation is staggering. The fruit, which was initially hardly recognisable, fills out and swells, just because there is sap rising. The vine will in fact send its roots deep enough to reach the water table in order to stay alive and thrive.

So for ourselves how do we get our embryonic 'fruit' to grow? Well it won't be by looking at ourselves and getting tense and worried about how we are doing, but thankfulness will, in a mysterious way, bring fruitfulness. I think that as we thank Him for His life flowing to us and through us, it's like putting those roots down deep and letting the 'water of life' from our Saviour rise up, making the fruit grow naturally.

If we spend time thanking Him for the wonderful privilege of having His life flow through us, rather than trying to squeeze out some more fruit to satisfy ourselves that we are OK then that life, I believe, will flow more freely and powerfully.

Activation ...

So next time a situation challenges your 'fruit bearing ability' turn your heart to Him and thank Him that you are in Him, and that He is in you. Thank Him for the flow of life coming from Him through you and you might be surprised at what happens next. Life with Jesus is so much more fun this way!

DAY 68 | Thanksgiving that God is in the ordinary

The story of Ruth is such a lovely one. It's a story we can read and enjoy for its joyous ending and happy outcome for all the main characters. There was the big moment, which is often written and preached about, when she tells Naomi not to try to persuade her to go back to her people. The moment when she declares that she has made up her mind, and she is going to stay with Naomi, belong to her people, and to her God. (Ruth 1:16).

Today however, it is the ordinary things that Ruth did, in virtual obscurity, that have taken my attention, because Ruth didn't just make the big gesture, she followed it up with faithful, but relatively mundane, service with no spotlight on her, and no hope of any earthly reward.

We know the story, how Ruth a Moabite, married into an Israelite family after they had immigrated to Moab from Bethlehem, during a time of famine. The family hits tragedy and all the men, namely her husband, father in law and brother in law, die leaving the three women to fend for themselves. Naomi, Ruth's mother in law, decides to go back to her roots in Judah and Ruth sacrificially insists on going with her.

She chose the unglamorous route, away from the chance of a remarriage, as she went with Naomi in order to 'look after her' for the rest of her life. She then sets about working to feed them both. It was hard work too. Gleaning in the fields would have been back breaking, for very long hours and very hot work. It was also work that could be dangerous for an unattached woman. In other words she chose to serve in the everyday and ordinary tasks of life, away from any human praise or affirmation.

The point I am making is this; Ruth had no status, power, prestige, fortune or anything else to make her stand out from the millions of other young women who have lived similar lives, and yet her story has been written to encourage us all. As far as Ruth was concerned she was an unknown widow, doing an unspectacular job, caring for her mother-in-law, but our God 'saw' and was delighted with what He saw. No wonder He chose to put her, a gentile woman, into the genealogy of Jesus. (Matthew 1:5).

Ruth's story gives us a clue about what the Lord 'honours'. Just think, she lived in a small agricultural community several thousand years ago, even before the Israelites had a king. The best way I can visualise her world is from my school history books that described Anglo Saxon village life, though of course Ruth lived nearly a thousand years before that time. She cared, she served, and she worked hard.

She was like so many unsung heroes and heroines who just get on with life and do their best to care for others along the way. I believe that in heaven all our stories are noted and recorded, and it may be that all our stories will be told too. What we do know is that there is a cloud of witnesses cheering us on, (Hebrews 12:1), and we know that the whole of creation is waiting for the manifestation of the sons (and daughters) of God. (Romans 8:19). It matters in heaven therefore how we live and what we do when no one seems to be looking.

Activation . . .

Today if your life seems full of the mundane and ordinary, consider Ruth and, thank God today that He is in the ordinary and the everyday. As you look to 'bear much fruit', thank Him for His presence with you, because if He is with you, then whatever you are doing, every moment becomes a holy moment, and a chance to delight your Heavenly Father who 'sees' from heaven when no one else does.

DAY 69 | Thanksgiving that 'we are not alone'!

I was intrigued recently by an article in the paper. It was provoked by the Nasa mission to Mars and the quest to find some sign of microbiological life using the Rover Perseverance. The writer {Rod Liddle, The Sunday Times, February 21st 2021} wrote that, 'after 50 missions, there is probably not a hope of that happening'. He also pointed out that the maths has significantly narrowed, in the search for extra terrestrial life.

Initially it was thought that, in Nasa's search for extra terrestrial life, that there could be between 1,000 and 100,000,000 possible life supporting planets in the Milky Way, but now some of the latest work from Oxford University in 2021 suggests that, because of some "bizarre revolutionary transitions" that have occurred on earth, we are probably alone!!!!

The desperate quest mankind is on to find something, or someone 'out there!' intrigues me. May be this quest is because, if we **are** all alone in the universe, it is quite a frightening thought. If we are just one human race on the only habitable, but tiny, planet anywhere in the universe, and as a species find ourselves constantly struggling with greed and power and behavior which threatens the future of the planet and mankind itself, then that is scary.

Given the size and magnificence of the universe that knowledge can make mankind feel lonely, isolated, and scared that there is no alternative place for us to go, and no other greater, or more benevolent being to come and rescue us from ourselves. Oh but wait!! May be there is!!

Today I find myself thanking God that we are definitely, definitely 'not alone'. There are indeed extra terrestrials and they are called 'angels'. Furthermore they don't want to abduct us but they come and help us as we journey through our life on earth. (Hebrews 1:14). According to Revelation 5:11 there are myriads of myriads of them, i.e. an indefinable and great number.

Over the last 4,000 years there have been many 'sightings' of these beings by a great variety of different people, many of them recorded in the Bible.

We also know that they are able to intervene in world events. Daniel 10:12-14, and Daniel 12:1-3, give us a tantilising glimpse into what happens when heaven's plans invade the plans of men on the earth. So we can definitely thank God that we are not alone

Today however, I can feel an even bigger burst of gratitude rising in my heart, because we didn't have to spend millions of pounds, and years of research – as in the 2.8 billion dollars spent on the mission to Mars – to find God. Put simply He didn't wait for us to find Him, the overwhelming truth is that Jesus came to earth to find us.

Paul wrote to the church in Philippi that 'Jesus Christ, who, being in very nature of God, did not consider equality with God something to be grasped, but made Himself nothing, taking the very nature of a servant . . . humbled Himself and became obedient to death – even death on a cross.' Philippians 2:6-8.

Activation . . .

God wanted connection with us and, perhaps that desire for connection with other life forms is in fact a manifestation of the hunger that God put in man for connection with Himself. Whether or not that is so, join me today in thanking the Lord that He came. In the words of Mark Altrogge's beautiful song . . .

'You did not wait for me to draw near to you, but you clothed yourself in frail humanity. You did not wait for me to cry out to you but you let me hear Your voice calling me. And I'm forever grateful to you, I'm forever grateful for the cross; I'm forever grateful to you, that you came to seek and save the lost.'

DAY 70 | Thanksgiving for those we meet

When Jesus sent His disciples into the world to spread His Kingdom, He gave them a plan to follow – and it was very simple. He said go where you are welcomed, accept the hospitality that is offered you, see what they need, release blessing into that need, and then you can tell them that the Kingdom of God is near. (Matthew 10:5-12). I think that these instructions, this template for connecting with people, is still very relevant to us today.

In today's society where people are more guarded we might not find ourselves invited into many homes People may well not know that we are followers of Jesus. In a sense, however, every interaction that we have with another person is like being inviting into their world.

The encounters that we have with people may be very brief with, for example, the postal delivery person, or the cashier at the supermarket. Other encounters may be longer, like a more significant interaction with our neighbours, and then we have those more significant times in our homes with family and friends. How ever long the encounter is, and we may only just see into a small part of the person's world, we can still see it the Jesus way – as an opportunity to build some level of relationship and so release a blessing.

Jesus plan still stands, especially if we can see it as an honour to be able to cross the threshold into someone's life, (even if just into the hallway metaphorically speaking), and can accept their hospitality at whatever level they set it. If we can thank the Lord in our hearts for them and for this moment where our lives connect, we may well find that our warmth and friendliness opens the door to a conversation where we see that they have a need that we can meet, or something for which we can pray.

Unlike in Jesus' day, free health care, and the availability of good drugs may mean that the person we meet may not have sickness in their family, (though often they do have), but they might have loneliness, or worries that we can address with our prayers and actions. The equivalent of the disciples 'healing the sick' could be simply looking to bring the Kingdom of God into their situation by blessing them as the Lord leads.

Personally I have often been challenged by those gifted ones who move dramatically in 'words of knowledge' and 'the prophetic'. They talk with strangers on a plane, or in a shop, and see them dramatically healed, or set free from some oppression. If you're like me, you might then easily write yourself off as an effective ambassador for our wonderful Saviour, so maybe we need to be open to a whole variety of gifting that can bless.

It could be to take some nourishing homemade soup to a neighbor who has lost all appetite, or some flowers to the one who has lost a love one. Then if our gift and blessing is received we can tell them in whatever way seems appropriate, that the Kingdom of Heaven has come near, that God cares about them and loves them.

Whatever we feel about ourselves as carriers of the gospel, and however bold we feel, my experience has been that if I can start by thanking God in my heart for those connections that occur with different ones during the day I am more likely, as I welcome them into my life – even for a moment, to sense the nudges of the Holy Spirit to open up conversations and to be able to bless them.

We live in a very secular society and need to follow the Holy Spirit's leading as we take our Good News out into the world. But 'take it out' we must, because the world sadly is less and less inclined to come to us.

Activation . . .

Take time to intentionally thank the Lord for the friend, neighbour, or stranger that you next meet by chance. As you do listen out for the promptings of the Holy Spirit as to what question you can ask that might give you that brief invitation 'into' their life and the opportunity to bless.

DAY 71 | Thanksgiving that God's Kingdom is forever

I was struck this morning by the words at the end of the Lord's Prayer – **'forever and ever. Amen'**. I guess I've always been excited by the previous words, **'Yours is the Kingdom and the Power and the Glory'** – especially when praying into a difficult situation- and I've not really dwelt on those last few words, **'forever and ever. Amen'**. It's a phrase that resonates with the words that Jesus spoke to John on the Isle of Patmos, "I am the living one: I was dead, and behold I am alive forever and ever." Revelation 1:18.

In the last few years so much that we have taken for granted has been shaken in the world politically, economically and socially. So many people are wondering what the future holds 'post Brexit', 'post Covid' and with the fallout from the war in Ukraine. These things have all affected people in terms of their finances, their social interactions, and therefore their mental health, and as a consequence their family life.

Sometimes we can find ourselves wondering 'where and when will it all end?' It can feel like everything is changing very fast, and not always for the better. So many things that we thought that our governments had under control, now seem way beyond them.

Today I believe the Lord would say to those of us who are feeling worried by all the uncertainties, whether for ourselves, our family, our nation, or our world, "It is time to lift your gaze to heaven, and see who is on the throne." And the good news is that the Lamb is on the throne and He will be there **forever and ever'**. Revelation 5:13.

As an antidote to our fears, we can thank God today that we are part of a Kingdom that will not pass away, and we can thank God that 'Jesus is the same yesterday, today and forever.' Hebrews 13:8. We can thank Him that 'He Is the Alpha and Omega,' the beginning and the end. (Revelation 1:8). We have an unchanging God, and we can thank the Lord that He is, and always will be, seated on the throne, **forever and ever.**

I think of those beautiful words that Trish and Noel Richards wrote in 1987,

'All heaven declares the glory of the risen Lord.
Who can compare with the beauty of the Lord?
Forever He will be, the Lamb upon the throne,
I gladly bow the knee and worship Him alone'.

The whole of heaven is echoing that refrain, 'Blessing and Honour and Glory and Power, be to Him who sits on the throne; and to the Lamb **forever and ever.'** And having heard that we just have to join the four living creatures, and elders who worship and say 'Amen', (Or as it is put in The Message; 'The four … fall down and call out 'Oh Yes!') Revelation 5:13,14.

So now when we think of the Lord's prayer in the context of our changing world, let us thank Him that when He was on earth He gave us those two phrases coupled together so that we can say them with one breath, **'Yours is the Kingdom and the Power and the Glory, forever and ever Amen'.** They belong together and form the unchanging truth that in changeable times we have an unchanging God, **'forever and ever, Oh yes!'**

Activation . . .

Next time you feel worried about 'where it's all going'! Thank the Lord again that He is on the throne of heaven, forever and ever!! In fact don't wait until you are worried, thank Him daily for this wonderful truth and it will always lift your eyes to see where your daily help comes from.

My help comes from the Lord the Maker of heaven and earth.

The Lord will watch over your coming and going both now and forevermore.

Psalm 121:2 and 7.

DAY 72 | Thanksgiving that it's His kingdom, His Power and therefore His Glory

Yesterday, we were looking at the amazing truth that God's Kingdom will last forever and ever. We were thanking God for this truth that can make the uncertainties, and all the changes that are happening all around us in our world today, far less threatening,

In that same prayer Jesus also told His disciples to pray to the Father for this 'Kingdom that will last forever' to come to earth, and for His will to be done on earth as it is in heaven. His words still stand for us today and, lest we should feel completely overwhelmed in the increasingly secular society in which we live, it is worth remembering that those words were first spoken to a people who lived in a land occupied by a very brutal and very pagan empire.

I think God is speaking in these days to those of us who feel powerless to stop some of the destructive things that are happening around us in our world. Things like the secularisation of many areas of life, the political correctness that threatens to silence the Christian voice, and the unleashing of unpleasantness (the works of the flesh Galatians 5:19-21) in so many different ways via the internet.

I am reminded of Gideon and how he must have felt, living in a time when Israel was in chaos. The faith and values of those who sought to follow Yahweh were threatened from within the nation by false religion, and without by the pagan Midianite invaders. Gideon is called by God to 'deliver' his people, but the opinion he had of himself was that he was 'the least in his family and his clan the least in his tribe of Manassah'. Judges 6:15.

When it came to it, the Lord was so faithful to Gideon and we read that before the first battle, 'the Spirit of the Lord came upon Gideon', Judges 6:34. The word used here indicates that, in effect, the Spirit 'clothed him'. That same Spirit came upon the disciples at Pentecost and 'clothed them with power from on high.' Luke 24:49. This happened at various times throughout the Acts of the Apostles, and we see how when the Holy Spirit came upon the disciples they were emboldened to pray and speak and preach in a hostile world. Acts 4:31.

Now God might not be telling us, as He did Gideon, that He is going to save our whole nation through our efforts, but I believe each one of us is positioned in a family, a neighbourhood, a church, or among friends and colleagues, and the Lord is saying to us as He did to Gideon, "the Lord is with you mighty warrior, go in the strength you have". Judges 6:14

I believe that the Lord wants us to know that, however small we feel in the face of all that is happening in our world, we are asked to pray to a very, very mighty God, and if like Gideon those prayers lead us to take action, the Lord will also fill us with His Spirit and 'clothe us' in His power. Our wonderful helper the Holy Spirit will enable us and give us boldness.

Activation . . .

Today thank God that it is not by might, or by being humanly powerful, but by His Spirit that His Kingdom will come on earth where we are. Let us thank God as we pray those words, "Your Kingdom come, Your will be done", that we are never asked to face anything alone, that it is His Kingdom and that it is also His power to bring in that Kingdom, and so all the Glory will be His too.

DAY 73 | Thankfulness, that our God is patient

I am increasingly thankful in these days that our God is so very patient. It is a beautiful quality and one that we do well to recognise as we seek to walk with Him day by day.

How do we know that He is patient? Well it is one of the nine fruits of the Spirit, and so if it is something that the Holy Spirit takes the trouble to develop in us, then it must also be a significant characteristic of God our loving Father. We also read that patience is the first attribute of love as they are listed for us in 1 Corinthians 13. (That list, incidentally, written out for us in verses 4 to 8 of 1 Corinthians 13, is actually a wonderful summation of the kind of love that God has for us.)

Jesus took the trouble to let His hearers know that God is very patient when He told the story of 'The Prodigal Son', Luke 15:11-31. Jesus tells us that while the son is taking his time, and it sounds like a reasonably long time, 'coming to his senses', the father was waiting and watching. We know this because we are told, 'his Father saw him while he was a long way off'. He was patiently waiting for his son to return, so that he could run and get to him first. His desire was to restore his son and maybe to prevent the elders of the village from banishing him forever.

We catch a similar picture of the Lord in Isaiah 30, when God speaks through the prophet to His rebellious people. The ones of whom He says 'These are a rebellious people, deceitful children, children unwilling to listen to the Lord's instruction' verse 9. Then after this description of their waywardness, He says 'therefore will the Lord wait, that He may be gracious to you, and therefore He will be exalted that He may have mercy upon you', verse 18 (from the AV).

Even though the nation was under judgment, the Lord was patiently waiting, giving them time to repent and find His mercy. This would mean that they could again be a blessed people, in the same way that the prodigal son was blessed by being forgiven and totally reinstated as a beloved son.

These passages from both the Old and New Testaments are surely showing us the heart of our loving Heavenly Father, who waits patiently for us to come to Him, whether that is for help in a situation, or to turn away from stuff that isn't doing us any good, or to simply catch onto the things that He is wanting to teach us. His patience shows us that He believes in us and His new life within us, even when we don't always believe ourselves.

For many of us impatience is far more natural than patience. We live in a world that is instant, and we become accustomed to high speed everything. We recently restarted an old computer that we 'neglected' for a newer model. I couldn't believe how long it took to load. I can get so impatient with things that don't deliver instantly and, if you're like me, you may find that it is also easy to be impatient not just with technology, but with ourselves and with other people too.

It is important then that we don't project that impatience onto God. It is all too easy for the enemy to tell us that God is probably totally fed up with us, and that He is getting very impatient with our slowness to learn.

Activation . . .

Today remind yourself of the nature of God by thanking Him for His patience with you, and also that

'His loving kindness is better than life', Psalm 63:3. AV.

You can also help yourself to grow in **your** patience by thanking Him for **His** patience. Thank Him too for those people and situations in your life at the present time that may be 'trying' **your** patience in some way!! As you thank the Lord for placing them in your life, the fruit of the Spirit that is 'patience' will grow.

It's a wonderful key to becoming daily more like Him.

DAY 74 | Thanksgiving for our differences

It is so easy in life to notice difference isn't it? Sometimes 'difference' can be very threatening. It can even lead us to judge or criticise others. When those differences are within our own community however, be that church, work, family, or peer group and those people who are different to us are the ones we admire, it can lead us to compare ourselves unfavourably and as a consequence feel negatively about ourselves.

So often if there is any 'difference' we end up measuring ourselves against that other person. We can see them as better as or worse than us, higher or lower, OK or not OK, and we don't like to feel that we are not in the OK group, whatever that might be. In the church this can be difficult as we can look at a fellow believer, whom we admire, and think 'well I ought to be like him (or her)' and undervalue the things about ourselves that make us different.

The truth is that God **made** us all different. We have different personalities, different gifts and talents, different backgrounds and education, sometimes even different priorities, and we need to thank God for that variety. While we know that the Holy Spirit is working in us all to make us more like Jesus, and that we are also encouraged to 'imitate the **faith**' of those who lead us, (Hebrews 13:7), God is not wanting us all to become clones, or carbon copies of one another.

Instead of comparing ourselves, which can lead to us positioning ourselves and others on an imaginary ladder, thereby imputing relative value to each one, we need to celebrate our differences and look for differences in others that we can value. I like the picture that Keith Green painted for us in His song 'Colours of the Rainbow', where he sees us, God's children, as pieces of stained glass in a window. As Jesus shines through us all, while it is His light, we all reflect very different colours.

The words are, 'We are the colourful ones, we are God's daughters and sons'. Now if Christ is shining through us and the colour coming through each of us looks very much the same, it could be because we are dirty or opaque, so that we are all giving off a dull murky colour. Being changed to be like Jesus, on the contrary, could mean that our differences will become more obvious, because if we are clean and clear, as the Lord shines through us, the different colours will be brighter and sharper, and the contrast between us all the greater.

God wants us to be like a kaleidoscope of colour, reflecting all the different aspects of His creativity. He wants us to become like Jesus, but does not want the wrong kind of sameness. Look at those twelve apostles for example, such a diverse bunch and each one called and chosen to be a founding pillar of the church. There has got to be difference, or else we will not be fully able, as a group of people, to fully represent our amazing many faceted God.

I think Paul sums it up in Romans 12:1-11 – definitely worth a read. He is encouraging the Christians to use their different gifting in the most Christ like way that they can, and to use that gifting, that talent, to serve each other. Like those early Christians let us also 'offer our bodies as a living sacrifice to God', Romans 12:1, thanking Him, with a whole heart, for the person that He has made us to be.

As we thank Him we can, with the Holy Spirits indwelling help, then set about becoming the best and most Christ like version of 'us' that there can be. We can also thank God that He made others different to us, and then our unity and oneness will be in that we are all manifesting the beautiful character of Jesus through our God given uniqueness.

Activation . . .

As you thank God today for who He has made you to be, ask the Holy Spirit to show you how you can grow in manifesting the fruit of the Spirit through the very unique person that you are so that you become, increasingly, one of His beautiful 'colourful ones'!

DAY 75 | Thanksgiving that our God is the Prince of Peace

It is fascinating to me that in our increasingly secular society, there is nevertheless a deep hunger for many of the attributes of our God. I was thinking today about 'peace', and what a high value is placed on finding peace in our busy and frenetic world. Now there are many different uses for the word 'peace'. It can sometimes mean an absence of hostilities, as in a physical war, or even a war of words. Then we can also use the word 'peace' to conjure up an internal state of calm and freedom from worry – 'peace of mind'.

In whatever context the word is used, it often conveys something that is highly desired by many individuals and people groups. It also something that seems very hard to find. Most often people try to find peace by removing the things that disturb their peace, or they may remove themselves from situations that threaten their peace. They may avoid conflict, or just bury or silence the voices that bring them disquiet by using drugs or distraction.

Wonderfully, we know that our God is in fact the source of real peace. 'Peace' emanates from Him, so no surprise then that when the prophet Isaiah heralds the wonderful arrival of the Messiah on earth he says that He will be called 'The Mighty God' and also 'the Prince of Peace' (Isaiah 9:6). And Jesus, our Prince of Peace', came into what was, at the time, a far from peaceful world.

It isn't the only time God identifies Himself as the one who brings peace into fraught situations. In Judges 6:7-24, Gideon was questioning his visitor, thinking that he was an angel, about all the trouble that the Israelites were having with the Midianites. He was asking whether God had abandoned His people. He then realised that he was in fact talking to the Lord and he panicked, expecting to die. At that point the Lord says "Peace! Don't be afraid. You are not going to die". Clearly peace came to Gideon with these words from the Lord and so he builds an altar and calls it 'Jehovah Shalom' – The Lord is Peace'.

From both these passages we learn that God, when He comes, brings peace into a troubled world, or a troubled situation. It is notable that in both of those instances He doesn't remove the problem but brings who He is, 'Jehovah Shalom', right into the world with all its turmoil. He comes as the Prince of peace into Roman occupied Israel and to Gideon in the middle of his war with the Midianites.

I think we are often deceived into thinking that peace will come to us if we can put an end to the things that disturb or worry us. We hope that peace will come when those things stop. Unfortunately focusing on trying to avoid, or stop, those things that disturb our peace can simply make things worse. Peace is actually something we can have because we have the Prince of Peace living in our lives. He is the bringer of the real peace that displaces our worries, fears and unrest. He wants to give us His peace in the midst of everything else, **even before** what is troubling us goes away.

Paul described this as 'the peace of God which transcends all understanding', and which will 'guard your hearts and your minds in Christ Jesus'. Philippians 4:7. So today rather than fight our fears, worries and anxieties, let us turn to the Lord and thank Him that His peace is an invading kind of peace, that it displaces fear, worry and disquiet. Thank Him that we don't have to wait for all the wars, both in our inner and outer world, to cease, but that we can invite Him 'The Prince of Peace' into any part of our lives where there is a lack of peace.

Activation . . .

Give thanks today very specifically that He is **your** Jehovah-Shalom, as you offer up to Him those areas of life where you are needing 'peace', and discover that it is His life in you that is your true source of real peace.

DAY 76 | Thanksgiving that we are called to be peacemakers

Yesterday we were thanking the Lord that He is our wonderful 'Prince of Peace' who brings His 'Shalom' into our lives. Today we are looking at the amazing truth that we, as God's children, are called to carry that peace into our sore and hurting world. In what we call 'the sermon on the mount' Jesus said 'Blessed are the peacemakers for they will be called the children of God'. That's us!! As God's children we now share His spiritual DNA. We can carry His peace and so we get to be known as the children of God.

We are talking here about 'peacemakers' not 'peacekeepers'. This is important because, as we know, although peacekeepers can do a great deal of good sometimes, as we saw years ago in Sarejevo, where the UN peacekeeping force had no authority to stop a massacre, peacekeepers may be powerless to prevent trouble. It can be the same for us if 'keeping the peace' just results in us being passive and ineffective.

Peace**makers**, the kind Jesus is talking about here are, I believe, going to be those who have seen that 'peace' is a weapon of warfare. It is something we can use actively against the pain and chaos that the enemy seeks to release into our world. If we look at the soldiers armory in Ephesians 6:10-17 we see that the feet – for advancing – are fitted with the gospel of peace. Bringing peace to someone, or some situation, by how we act, speak, or pray in His name is a very significant part of our warfare in this life.

As we noted yesterday, the 'shalom' peace of God is not an absence of trouble but it is, in fact, the powerful presence of God released into a situation. As His 'Ekklesia', His representatives on earth, we have that authority to move in against the enemy however he is manifesting himself. In Matthew 16:18, we read that Jesus has given His followers the authority to bind and loose whatever has been already bound or loosed in heaven. We are called, in fact, to partner on earth with our Prince of Peace now reigning in heaven.

Jesus primarily bought peace between God and mankind through a gruesome death on the cross. The Hebrew word shalom, however, used in Isaiah 9:6, also carries the sense of total wellbeing, of welfare, health, and prosperity in addition to peace. The Lord now gives us, His children, His authority to bring to others that offer of peace with God, and the authority also, I believe, to destroy enemy strongholds that are destroying peace and wellbeing in many different ways here on earth. He gives us spiritual weapons that 'have divine power to demolish strongholds.' 2 Corinthians 10:4. This 'peace' is powerful and we are called as peacemakers to release this peace into our world.

Our thanksgiving today is that we, those of us who are 'in Christ', have this incredible privilege of being carriers of God's peace into our world. We are bringers of peace, and whether that is between nations, or neighbours, church members, colleagues, friends or family members, we are not powerless in the face of all that the enemy does to destroy peace in this world. We can thank the Lord that far from being overcome by the atmospheres all around us, we are atmosphere changers as we release the peace that He imparts to us into the world around us.

Activation . . .

Join me today in saying 'Thank you Jesus for the privilege and the adventure of partnering with you in this way, please increase my faith and effectiveness as I walk with you. Amen'.

Then give thanks when you find yourself in situations where peace is needed, and release the peace of God by your words, declaration, prayer, or actions as the Holy Spirit directs.

DAY 77 | Thanksgiving for the gift of 'Today'

The psalmist in Psalm 118:24 writes, 'This is the day that the Lord has made; let us rejoice and be glad in it'. It sounds so simple doesn't it? So often however the joy and rejoicing in our 'today' is spoilt by intrusive thoughts about my 'yesterdays', concerns for 'today' itself, and worries about my 'tomorrows'.

The fact is that there is only one 'today' for us, and that is the twenty four hours we are presently living through. It's a precious span of time that can never be repeated and which has its own unique challenges and opportunities. It is twenty four hours in which we want to live fully alive to all that the day presents us with, and fully aware of the Lord's presence with us.

Now looking back can be good if the past helps us to enjoy today by filling us with hope and expectations, but other thoughts from the past are harder to handle and can prevent us from fully engaging with our 'present'. These can include worries and regrets about what we have, or haven't done well. If we feel that we have messed up for example, we can even find it hard to let go and forgive ourselves and others.

We can also have unhealthy nostalgic feelings about the past, allowing ourselves to have unhelpful comparisons with our 'present'. The antidote, to such unhelpful intrusive thoughts is faith that God has covered all our sins, and that He will weave even our failures into His plans and purposes for us. We can thank Him for all that He has led us through and taught us, and also that He is faithfully 'growing' us up into Christ in all things. Ephesians 4:15.

So what about thoughts of the future that can affect our enjoyment of today? They will, not surprisingly, include the worries and concerns about what is ahead and if we, and those we love, are going to be alright. It's no wonder then that Jesus said "do not worry about tomorrow, for tomorrow will worry about itself", Matthew 6:34.

When Corrie Ten Boom, as a child, asked her Father how she will cope with any future suffering, he explains that God only gives us the grace that we need for today. Anticipating the future and how you will cope is like bringing tomorrow into today, without the supply of grace that will come with it. So, as we battle anxieties about the future, we can thank God as we 'cast every care onto Him,' 1 Peter 5:7, thank Him that 'He cares for us' and that He will be releasing grace for tomorrow when 'the tomorrow' comes.

Finally, we can lose our 'joy' in today, just by simply worrying if we will have what we need for the day – time, strength, money, patience, wisdom etc, etc. We need to thank God that 'His grace is always sufficient', 2 Corinthians 12:9, and that 'our strength will equal our days,' Deuteronomy 33:25, and so will everything else that we need too! (I like the NASB translation that reads, 'according to your days, so shall your leisurely walk be.')

Without being too dramatic, we will only have one shot at today, so let's give it our best, and thank the Lord that there is grace for everything that comes our way today. Our thanksgiving is like a shout of faith to our wonderful Heavenly Father, that He will supply all our need as we go through the day, that He is here with us in our present, that He has covered our past, and that there will be grace for our future. This, I believe, is how we can help ourselves towards 'rejoicing and being glad' in each and every day.

Activation . . .

Today thank the Lord every time those unhelpful thoughts come to rob you of your joy saying, "Lord I thank you that you have forgiven my past, I thank you that there will be grace for everything that comes my way in the future, and also I thank you for your 'all sufficient presence' that is with me today.

DAY 78 | Thanking God for every fresh challenge

By challenge here I am referring to anything that stretches our faith. Some challenges can be exciting, some daunting, all are within the permissive will of a loving heavenly Father who, throughout the scriptures, expresses His confidence in us His children over and over again. Well in fact He expresses His confidence in Christ in us, and in the Holy Spirit's equipping and leading of us through trials and difficulties.

Throughout the Bible there are many examples of God's people facing challenges that they felt, even knew, were beyond them and their own capacity to handle. How they received those challenges, particularly in respect of how they saw themselves and their resources as God's servants, was crucial to their success.

Let's look first of all at Joshua and Caleb and the ten spies when faced with the challenge of 'taking the Promised Land'. After having seen the size of the fortified cities and the giants Joshua and Caleb said, "We should go up and take possession of the land for we can certainly do it", the other ten said, in effect, 'no way' because "all the people there are of a great size ... We seemed like grasshoppers **in our own eyes**". Numbers 13:26-32. The end of that story is that Joshua and Caleb were the only two from those twelve who entered the Promised Land, albeit some forty years later.

How about David and Saul? They were both chosen and anointed to be Kings of Israel. The key to how they did is in how they saw themselves. One became famous for his success as King and the other dipped out badly after a good start. Saul was described as 'an impressive young man without equal among the Israelites, and a head taller than any of the others.' 1 Samuel 9:2. But when it was time to be anointed king, and inspite of having had an extraordinary experience of the power of God coming on his life (1 Samuel 10:9-11), he hid himself in the baggage (verse 22).

David on the other hand was mocked as a young upstart, but then without any armour, just his trust in the God who was with him and for him, slew the giant Goliath. He then survived being unjustly outlawed and became a great king. Saul is tall but afraid because he, like the ten spies, is small in His own eyes. David faced with a giant wasn't afraid, knowing that 'the battle is the Lord's.' 1 Samuel 17:47. And so we can see that how we see ourselves, in the light of God's promises to us, is so very important.

A good example of this truth is Gideon, who we have mentioned previously. He started off seeing himself as very small and insignificant and yet he 'hears' how God sees him and goes in the strength of the Lord and delivers Israel from the Midianites. Judges 6:15,16.

There are many other incidents, in both the Old and New Testaments, of people facing huge difficulties and finding that the Lord gives His people 'strength'. It is very noticeable that the ones who succeeded were the ones who chose to see themselves the way God saw them, and to see God as their strengthener and deliverer.

We know that Paul, for example, went through many trials for his faith before he wrote down his belief that we are to be 'more than conquerors through Him who loved us.' Romans 8:37. This same man also wrote, 'I can do everything through Him who gives me strength.' Philippians 4:13.

So what about us? I believe that if we can give thanks to God for both the challenges and the trials that come our way, we are in fact expressing our trust and confidence in who God has made us to be 'in Christ'. Thanksgiving for the situations in which we find ourselves gives voice to our faith that He will always be with us, and that He will enable us to walk in triumph

---

Activation . . .

Today give God thanks for every challenge facing you. Thanksgiving will bring you into agreement with the Lord about who you now are 'in Christ', and at the same time it will enable you to receive His strength and provision for all the challenges that come your way today.

DAY 79 | Thanksgiving that He gives us strength

Yesterday we were looking at how giving thanks in all of life's challenges can help us to see ourselves as God sees us. Thanksgiving for the situations that we are in positions us to believe that God has confidence in us because of the life of Christ in us. Giving thanks also helps us to remember that He has given us the Holy Spirit to indwell us and to be our helper. We said that our gratitude expresses our openness to God to receive the Holy Spirit's help and all of God's provision to cope with the challenges before us.

We were considering people in the bible who faced epic challenges like leading a nation, or an army, things beyond the experience of most of us. We too can have big battles, and as you read this you may be in the midst of a major challenge in your life. Often times the things confronting us are the more everyday ones like family relationships, finances, things in our work or church life, or the need for provision, direction and guidance.

I think the Lord wants us to recognise that, even if the challenges facing us don't seem very big in the grand scheme of things, He still wants to help us with them. He wants to help us also with the things that come our way in our ordinary everyday lives. Things like managing our time, keeping our attitudes good, being patient and kind etc. He wants to help us to walk with Him in triumph in all the situations that come in our day to day lives.

My mother used to have an expression 'Give me strength!' She would say it whenever anything trying came her way. It was more an expression of exasperation than a prayer, and it would often come out over relatively trivial things, sometimes mere irritations. It is nevertheless interesting that the thing most of us want, when we are feeling out of our depth in a situation, is an infusion of energy – 'strength'- because unless we have the energy we will not be able to turn our creative, or practical, solutions into action.

We quoted some words yesterday from Philippians 4:13. Paul's declaration of the Lord's strength there for him in various and differing situations. The more literal Greek translation here in fact reads, 'All things I can do in the one *empowering* me'. I love it! The thought that God is 'empowering me' is quite energising in itself. We often see adverts that tell us with pride that something is 'powered' by some famous brand of engine, or processor. It conveys to us a sense that this item is so much more than it looks. And so are we, since we are 'powered' by the indwelling Holy Spirit ...

In another verse with which we can encourage ourselves, 2 Corinthians 12:9, Paul tells us that the Lord spoke to Him and said 'My grace is sufficient for you, my *strength* is made perfect in weakness.' The Greek word used here for strength is 'dunamis', the word from which we get our word dynamite. Paul continues (and again I am using a literal translation from the Greek) 'I will boast in the weakness in order that might overshadow over me the *power*'. That word 'dunamis' again conveying to us that something wonderfully supernatural is taking place in his life.

When the Lord offers us His strength, it is His 'dunamis'. It is more than physical strength, it is His enabling energy. So as we continue our journey of thanksgiving in the face of various challenges, let us expect an infusion of His miraculous strength and power. The Lord wants to enable us, to not just rise to the challenge in front of us, but to enjoy partnering with Him as we live our ordinary lives as supernaturally strengthened 'overcomers'.

Activation . . .

As you give thanks in the face of each and every challenge today, expect to receive the 'dunamis' of God in fresh ways that may well surprise you.

DAY 80 | Thanksgiving for the gift of choice

I wonder if it has ever crossed your mind what an incredible thing **choice** is, and just what a wonderful thing God did when He gave us the gift of **choice**. I don't know that if I was God, and I had just created a magnificent universe with this one small, but stunning, habitable planet as a home for these living created beings – 'humankind', that I would then give this creature the ability to make **choices.**

The gift of **choice** sets us apart from the animals who work by learning and instinct in order to survive. It is part of our being 'made in the image of God' Genesis 1:26, and it gives us a dignity the animals don't have. The gift of choice involves us having a conscience, being able to explore options, visualise outcomes, and even act sacrificially. Having 'choice' gives us opportunities both to plan and to act in good ways and bad. We get to be decision makers; there is no coercion with God.

Choice is an incredible gift to give anyone, but for God to do that, knowing that it would involve Him coming to our planet, in the same form as the people He had created, in order to pay the price for all the bad choices that they have, and will ever make, is simply mind blowing. God so wanted relationship with creatures who could choose to be in that relationship with Him, that He planned ahead of time to send Jesus to be our 'sacrificial Lamb'. No wonder there is such celebration over those who make it their choice to follow Him. Luke 15:7.

The wonderful thing is that, having made our choice to follow Him, we still have the ongoing gift of choice. He does not now program us to obey His every wish, or command, like robots. Relationship is still of the utmost importance to the Lord, and His desire is to lead us through life as a Father and friend. He wants us to grow in our desire to please Him, to learn how to discern His will, and to fellowship with the beautiful Holy Spirit, enjoying life as we go.

How often do we say to ourselves something like, "I don't know what to do", "I can't decide", and "I wish I didn't have to make a choice"? Well next time we hear ourselves struggling to know what to do in a situation, let us turn our hearts to Him and just thank Him for the gift of choice. He wants to be involved in our choices and for us to grow into 'having the mind of Christ.' 1 Corinthians 2:16. Turning in our hearts to thank Him when we have a choice to make, is a way of including Him in those choices and growing in our relationship with Him.

Let us thank Him every day that He didn't create a world and fill it with dutiful robots, but He gave us the gift of 'life' and with it the gift of 'choice'. Let us thank Him too that He came to 'seek and save the lost', Luke 19:10, to save us from the consequences of our bad choices. We can also thank Him that He wants to be involved in all our choices; the big life changing choices, and small day to day ones. He loves us and wants our friendship with Him to grow in every choice that we make, and when we really 'get' that, then making choices starts to get exciting.

Activation ...

Today as we thank God for the gift of choice we can agree with Paul as he declares ...

'This resurrection life you received from God is not a timid grave-tending life. It's adventurously expectant, greeting God with a childlike "What's next Papa?" God's Spirit touches our spirit and confirms who we really are.' (The Message.)

DAY 81 | Thanksgiving for His commandments

We wrote yesterday about the wonderful gift of choice that the Lord has given mankind, but I can imagine that someone might say, "Yes, but then He gave the Ten Commandments and took away our choice. We were given 'choice' and we don't now want to be told what to do and what not to do. We want the freedom to choose to do whatever we like".

I think if we look at the commandments more closely we can see that it was, in fact, an act of love on the part of God to give us these commandments through the nation of Israel. God knew that, since the devil's arrival on earth, mankind would inevitably be tempted to make some very bad choices, as did Adam and Eve. Through the Ten Commandments He gives mankind a golden template for right living, and a healthy society.

God was saying "You have freedom to choose, but you need some guidelines, so here are mine, you can't do better than follow them". If we look at them and imagine a society where everyone adhered to them, we can see that it would be a very good place in which to live. This is because they deal with all the selfishness that, in its many manifestations, spoils our world.

An 'expert of the law', who spoke to Jesus, understood this when he summed up the law in the words "Love the Lord your God with all your heart, and with all your soul, and with all your strength, and with all your mind, and love your neighbour as yourself." Luke 10:27.

Another question that might then be asked by a sceptic is, "If God has given us free choice why does He punish people for disobeying the rules He has set? Doesn't that negate the offer of choice?" Well, actually no!! He lets us know that we are free to choose, but also that there are consequences attached to every choice. 'Freedom to choose' does not equate with having everything I want, and nothing that I don't want.

So God, out of love for His people, also gave them a way to find forgiveness when they had failed to live as He wanted. This was so that they could come close to Him without being in big trouble. The Israelites had their sacrifices and detailed instructions on how to keep themselves 'cleansed' when they had 'sinned' by making bad choices, but God had something much better planned for us.

In Jeremiah 31:33 He said "I will put my law in their minds and write it on their hearts. I will be their God and they will be my people". We know that the fulfillment of that word is found in our new life in Jesus. He paid the price for all our sins, He writes His law on our hearts, and gives us the Holy Spirit as an indwelling guide, helping us to make good choices as we travel with through life.

Let us thank Him for His wisdom in not leaving us without guidance for our choices, and even more let us thank Him for writing His laws on our hearts and in our minds, and for giving us the Holy Spirit to help us to 'know' in our spirit what choices are pleasing to Him.

We now also have recorded for us, in the New Testament, a new and even harder commandment. The one that Jesus gave His followers, "to love one another as I have loved you." John 15:12. This new commandment seems even more impossible to keep, but wonderfully we have His new life within to help us live out even this amazing new commandment.

Activation . . .

Today meditate on the wonderful truth that, because of His indwelling presence, all His commands can become delightful to us, so that with the psalmist we can say "I love your commands more than gold". Wow! I do believe that the more we thank the Lord for His commands, by His grace we will grow and even learn to love our brothers and sisters in Christ in the way that He has loved us.

DAY 82 | Thanksgiving for the gift of repentance

As we think about the gift of choice given by God to mankind, we are going to look today at one more thing around this gift, for which we can be thankful. It is the gift of being able to change our minds. If we were not able to 'change our minds' we would find ourselves, once we had made our choice, locked into a course of action the consequences of which we might not have fully considered or understood. Making choices would be very hard, like walking a tightrope, and life would probably be rather full of regrets.

In the Bible God often asks people to 'repent', and repentance gets a bit of a bad press as it can be associated with a 'sackcloth and ashes'. (See Luke 10:13). Often times in the Old Testament, when there was conviction of sin people would tear their clothes, sit in sackcloth and smear themselves with ashes. (Joel 2:13). Repentance was associated with great grief, and even self flagellation.

The word 'repent' itself does not necessarily demand such emotion. The root of the word is about rethinking something, changing our minds, or our direction. There may well be strong emotions accompanying it, but as a Christian there can also be a lot of joy, because joy will come as we change our minds and line ourselves up with the way God is thinking about something. Then as our thinking changes so does our behaviour, and that pleases Him too.

After the second world war, Basilea Schlink, leader of an Evangelical Sisterhood based in Darmstadt Germany, wrote a book, 'Repentance the Joy filled Life'.* It was the first time I had heard the words repentance and joy in the same sentence, but she had unearthed a jewel for us all. She saw that repentance, which may be a sorrowful experience for a while, actually leads to joy. This is because Jesus paid the ultimate price for all our sins and so there is no judgement left for us, only the warm embrace of the Father when we turn back to Him from any wayward path that we have taken in thought, word, or deed. Basilea writes, 'Repentance – the gateway to heaven! Repentance – the way to the Father's heart and to overflowing joy!

Rob Des Cotes of the Imago Dei Christian Community, has also caught sight of the fact that repentance is not just about our initial turning to Christ, but about a lifestyle of getting closer and closer to Him. Rob writes, 'To know that you need to repent is, in itself, an insight from the Holy Spirit. To know it in an ongoing way is evidence of God's continued presence with us. It is a recurring gift that accompanies us along our whole earthly journey, purifying us as we go in thanksgiving for God's mercy.'

As we grow in Christ and learn to be more and more sensitive to the Holy Spirit, we will welcome His correction and enjoy His redirection because we will find ourselves drawing ever closer to the Lord. There is a strange joy, and indeed relief, in being 'turned around' by the Holy Spirit when we've forsaken His way of doing things. When we change our minds about a path that is not in accordance with His character and will, and choose His way it is like we have the wind under our sails again and we feel lighter and freer.

This gift of repentance is surely something for which we can thank God. Just knowing that at any time of the day or night I can turn to Him, 'change my mind' about something, and draw close to Him again is truly a wonderful gift. Our ongoing life of repentance is then a sign, not of failure, but that we are being transformed into His likeness little by little. (2 Corinthians 3:18).

A post script that I want to add today is this, when we feel that the Holy Spirit is pointing to something that needs changing in our lives, He will take us to Calvary, where we can find grace and forgiveness, and yes, joy. The enemy will condemn us and take us to Sinai, the law, our failure and condemnation. Don't go with him, stay looking to Calvary at all times and joy will be yours.

Activation . . .

Today thank Him for the wonderful truth that *'In repentance and rest is your salvation."* Isaiah 30:15 and prove it to be true.

Repentance the Joy Filled Life by Schlink, M. Basilea was republished by Evangelical Sisterhood Of Mary in January 2016

DAY 83 | Thanksgiving that our God loves to hear our voice

I guess the clue is in the first verse of John's Gospel where, we read 'In the beginning was the Word'. 'The Word' is of course Jesus. God, who is a great communicator, speaks to us through all that Jesus is and was, and all that He said and did. God also speaks through His written word the Bible and of course creation. Romans 1:20.

We have a speaking God, and one who created us, as spirit beings, capable of listening and hearing His voice, John 10:3. Our God is not however a dictator. He doesn't just give edicts from on high, or tell us 'keep quiet, listen to me, and do what I command'. The astonishing thing is that we have a God who loves two way communication; a God who gave us the gift of speech and who 'loves to hear **our** voice'. Song of Songs 2:14.

Over the years Mark and I have been involved with many people seeking to build better relationships with each other and, no surprise here, better communication has been one of the main keys in helping people achieve that goal. Using our voice and expressing to one another what is going on inside – our inner thoughts and feelings – in a safe and good way, can be life changing.

Some people are good at using their voice to say what they want, but then there are those who, for a variety of reasons don't use their voice. What they are thinking, feeling therefore stays hidden. This can be because they are afraid of the reaction they might get, or because they don't think that the other person is interested in what they have to say.

If that is the case, the relationship will be faltering badly, and sadly, for both parties. But what about us and God? Are we ever too afraid, or too ashamed to tell Him what is on our hearts, or maybe we feel there is no point, we are too insignificant, for Him to have time for us. We may just feel "Well He knows anyway there is no point. It's obvious what I need, maybe He just doesn't care". If we recognise any of those thoughts, then there are clearly some lies that we need to repent of believing, with the Holy Spirit's help! See Day 82.

Let us thank God today that we have a voice that He wants to hear, and a God who will listen and respond to us with kindness and compassion. He wants us to 'pour out our hearts to Him', Psalm 62:8. God can handle our perplexity, and even our anger, if we are coming, like Job, with a hope of finding comfort and resolution in our hearts. He won't be angry or upset but will help us to work out, for our good, what we bring to Him with our voice.

If the Lord does need to rebuke or correct us for what we 'pour out', it will be with love and an impartation of grace and, like Job, we could find ourselves saying, 'my ears had heard of you, but now my eyes have seen you', Job 42:5, because honest communication brings us closer to Him. No wonder that He loves to hear our voice.

One final word! We know that we can say whatever is on our hearts to Him, but remember that 'out of the overflow of the heart the mouth speaks.' Matthew 12:34. So let us make sure that our voice is sweet. Pouring out our heart in honesty is good but just grumbling and complaining is a sign of unbelief. So let us make sure that we are honouring Him with our lips by giving Him praise and thanks too.

Activation . . .

Approaching God with thanksgiving is so important and is, after all, what these daily meditations are all about. Heaven, where He dwells, is full of worship, so let all your communications today, with your wonderful Heavenly Father, be liberally sprinkled with your worship, thanksgiving and adoration. Like the Psalmist, you can pour out your heart to Him and also declare "I shall yet praise Him". Psalm 42: 11.

DAY 84 | Thanksgiving that with God there is 'fullness'!

People often ask if you are a 'glass half full', or a 'glass half empty' sort of person. The implication is that we are all looking at the same glass but some see things positively, by focusing on what is there, and others see things negatively, noticing what is not there. This is a reasonably good way of seeing whether someone is optimistic or pessimistic.

This can also apply to us as Christians. We can be glass half full, or glass half empty Christians. We can be aware, for example, of what we feel that God has done for us, or more aware of what He hasn't done yet. We can see how God has changed us over the years, or we can be more aware of what hasn't happened yet, and how we would love for things to be different. Sometimes progress in the Kingdom seems to be very slow!! It could apply to prayers answered or not; in fact any kind of change that we have been looking for, both in our external circumstances, or within our own character and person.

The good news is that God's purpose for us in Christ is **'fullness'**. Let's just look again at Paul's prayer for the Christians in and around Ephesus. He says "I pray that out of His glorious riches He may strengthen you with power through His Spirit in your inner being, so that Christ may dwell in your hearts through faith. And I pray that you being rooted and established in love, may have the power, together with all the saints, to grasp how wide and long and high and deep is the love of Christ, and to know this love that surpasses knowledge-that you may be filled to the measure of all the **fullness** of God." Ephesians 3:16-19.

Paul speaks 'of the glorious riches that we have in Christ' and even if we are not 'glass half empty people' we may still find ourselves focusing on what we lack in our walk with God. We can be looking at our weaknesses and failings, when we actually need to look at all that Christ is and wants to be in and for us. We need to see that every lack that we have is an opportunity to receive more of His grace, and His unchanging love for us.

Paul also wrote to those early Christians, 'Therefore if anyone is in Christ he is a new creation; the old has gone the new has come', 2 Corinthians 5:12. Becoming a Christian is not about joining a self improvement group. God, in effect says to us, "The old isn't working, it has to go, and I'm giving you a new life". No wonder Paul could also write, 'I am crucified with Christ, and I no longer live but Christ lives in me. The life I live in the body, I live by faith in the Son of God who loved me and gave Himself for me.' Galatians 2:20.

For every lack that you feel, God has a supply, and it is found in your 'new life in Christ'. Thanksgiving for the new will swallow up our negativity, doubts, and unbelief. It will take our focus off of the 'old us' and what isn't yet sorted, and help us to focus on the 'new person that we are in Christ' and on all that God has already poured into us and wants to pour into us. In God there is no 'half empty' as such, there is just opportunity for more growing as all our lack is swallowed up in His abundance.

So how does this work? Well, when I am tired and weary, I thank God that He is my strength, when I feel angry, I thank Him that He is my gentleness and patience. When I feel myself fretting, I thank Him that He is my peace. In fact as and when I become aware of a lack in myself, I can thank God that what I need can be found in my 'new life' in Christ. I can take my half, or even fully empty glass to God, and thank Him that He will, by His Spirit, release in me more of 'the measure of all the fullness of God' which is now mine 'in Christ.'

Activation . . .

Set your focus on your new nature in Christ today. Stop trying to renovate the old. He has made you a 'new creature', so when you become aware of a need (a half full moment) turn to Him with thanksgiving that whatever you need is already yours 'in Christ', and so live by faith from the life Christ has now put within you, because of His unfathomable love for you.

DAY 85 | Thanksgiving that we are 'rooted' in His love

We were planting some bare root trees recently, and as we looked at the incredible roots of these young trees it made me wonder about the remarkable job they were going to have to do if these trees were going to grow to their full height and grandeur. The roots are of course the means of so much nourishment coming into the tree system, but once planted they aren't seen, and they certainly aren't admired throughout all of the different seasons of the year, as are the leaves, the blossom and the fruit of the tree.

As we were planting yesterday, we were ensuring that the roots of the trees were going into good and well watered soil. In addition we were sprinkling something called mycorrhizal fungi onto the roots so that they would grow and thrive better and even be more able to cope with drought. In the passage we were looking at yesterday, part of the prayer that Paul prayed for the Christians in Ephesus was that they would be 'well rooted in love', Ephesians 3:17. I like that! He knew that how and where these Christians were rooted, was vital for their growth.

We know that we Christians, like trees, need good roots to stand strong in the storms and winds of life. We need strong roots that go down deep enough to find water in a drought, and it would seem that Paul, inspired by the Holy Spirit, could think of no better substance to help our roots grow strong and deep than the Love of God. How important it is for us to be 'well rooted in love', our own Christian 'mycorrhizal fungi'.

If we are harbouring doubts about how much God really loves us, everything about our faith can get a bit rocky and become hard work, but if we are rooted in His love, we will find ourselves drinking in His goodness even in the tough and stormy times in life. If we are struggling, and feel that we are not growing as a Christian, maybe we need to go back and look at our roots and refresh ourselves again in God's never failing, never ending love.

The prophet Jeremiah had to do this. That poor man hit so much trouble and persecution, even as he sought to obey God and bring prophetic truth to his people. It got so bad that at times he really doubted God, and his own calling. He talks about his bitterness of soul in Lamentations 3, then he makes this wonderful statement, "yet this I call to mind and therefore I have hope: because of the Lords great love, we are not consumed, for His compassions never fail, they are new every morning, great is your faithfulness". (Verses 22,23)

We are reminded of this at Easter when we focus on Jesus death and resurrection, but we also need to take the time to do that in any season of the year or indeed of our lives. As we call to mind God's amazing love for us, we will be refreshing our 'roots' with His love, because it was nothing but love that brought Jesus to earth, John 3:16, and it was certainly the most extraordinary love that took Him to the cross. So should there be any question in your heart about God's love for you, take a fresh look at the cross. He really can't say 'I love you' any louder, or clearer, than that!

Activation . . .

Colossians 2:6,7 says, 'just as we received Christ Jesus as Lord' we should 'continue to live in him, rooted and built up in Him, strengthened in the faith as we were taught, and **overflowing with thankfulness'**. Today thank God again and again for His love as you look again at the cross, and as you do that, you will find yourself truly 'rooted in His love', in the best possible 'soil' for growing in your faith every day.

DAY 86 | Thanksgiving for the 'seasons'

Walking in the woods that we have nearby is always a delight for us, especially in the spring. I love watching the changes and the metamorphosis that takes place all around. I am so glad to live somewhere where the seasons are distinct and the change is dramatic. Winter to spring is probably the most startling of those changes when things that looked dead, suddenly and literally, 'spring' into life before our eyes.

Winter however is still such an essential part of the yearly cycle in our climate. So many hidden things are going on under the ground and within the trees and plants themselves, and I find myself getting quite excited as winter starts to come to an end, in anticipation of what is about to happen over the next month or so.

Our Christian lives also go through seasons. There are times of great growth like spring, times of maturing like summer, and times of great fruitfulness like our autumn. There are also, I believe, those bewildering winter seasons when not a lot seems to be happening and we find ourselves questioning our life and faith journey. Is it OK? Am I OK? In fact, as in nature itself, a great many things are probably happening; things of which we are almost unaware.

Sometimes in a 'winter season' we can get a bit panicky because of the lack of evidence that we are 'doing OK'. Thoughts like 'Where are the opportunities that I used to have? And, 'I don't seem to be bearing any fruit these days', go through our minds. Or even 'Life feels a bit barren at the moment. I used to know the sunshine of your love Lord, but I can't see through the mist and fog at the moment'.

In our winter seasons there can be less outward evidence of God's presence with us. We may feel there is no obvious growth and liveliness in our faith, a limited sense that we are maturing and difficulty in enjoying the Lord daily. There can be that feeling that our lives are not so fruitful as they once were.

I do believe that in these 'wintery' seasons it is important that we continue with our daily thanksgiving. Yes, we can certainly ask the Lord if there is anything we need to know, or correct in our walk with Him, but I think it is important that we don't overdo the introspection. Keeping a heart of thanksgiving, for anything and everything we can think of, is always good as this will help to keep us connected to the Lord and will help us to be in a place to hear any course correction from Him, should we need it.

As we intentionally give thanks in these times we may find ourselves searching the scriptures a little harder, listening more intently to messages, praying more often, and generally looking forward more eagerly to connecting with the Lord in any way that we can. We will therefore find that these are the times when our roots are actually growing and going down deeper into His love. It's the same process as for our trees in winter. When the tree is having a rest from producing leaves and fruit its roots are digging deep for water and nourishment, ready for the next season of growth.

If that feels like you then do thank the Lord that He is watching over you in this season. He has clearly said, "Never will I leave you, never will I forsake you." Hebrews 13:5. He is so glad you are 'digging deeper' to find Him, to find more of His love and the sustenance that He has for you. Thank Him especially that He is preparing you for times of great fruitfulness ahead.

Activation . . .

Let your 'thanksgiving' help you not to waste time and energy wondering what has gone 'wrong', instead let it enable you to gain maximum 'root' growth during this time, for however long the Lord has you in this season.

DAY 87 | Thanksgiving for our certainties

One odd fact of 'life' is that, here on earth, physical death is the only real certainty that we have. It is interesting therefore, given that that is the case that people love to work with certainties in our modern world. We want to have the certainty that our money is safe and that internet fraud is not going to be allowed to empty our accounts. We even want to be certain what the weather will be like before we book holidays, or venture out for the day. It seems that for many people for life to 'go well' and peacefully, there is a need for certainty.

I wonder if that is why the recent covid pandemic hit the western world so hard. Suddenly all our certainties were shaken. The certainties that we could travel to where ever and whenever we wanted, and see whoever we wanted to whenever we wanted to, suddenly went. The certainty that doctors would have the answers for our illnesses, and that there would be an appointment to see a medical practitioner when necessary, disappeared. Even for us Christians the certainty that we could go to church wherever and whenever we wanted to, was gone. In fact that season was a good time for us as Christians to examine what certainties we really were relying on.

Our certainties come to us from God, and wonderfully, there are many certainties for us to thank God for in the spiritual world. The world systems can and will be shaken about by all sorts of things – physical, economic and political, but God's Kingdom cannot be shaken. Because of the cross and Jesus' resurrection God's Kingdom has been established and, unlike the kingdoms and empires on earth that all come and go with time, this Kingdom will keep on increasing. (Isaiah 9:7).

There are other great spiritual certainties which can undergird our lives when everything around us gets shaken. Spiritual certainties can't be seen but are certainly stronger than some of the things in which people put their faith on earth. 'Now faith is being sure of what we hope for and certain of what we do not see.' Hebrews 11:1. So here are some spiritual certainties for which we can thank the Lord; certainties that will undergird our whole lives; certainties that we can live by and which will give us peace in changing times, as we confess them and thank God for them daily.

1. Whatever else is happening in the world we know that one day we will be able to say that "The Kingdom of this world **has** become the Kingdom of our God and of His Christ, and He **will** reign forever and ever." Revelation 11:15

2. This same Jesus will never turn us away when we come to Him. 'Whoever comes to me I will **never** drive away.' John 6:37. God has said '**never will I leave you; never will I forsake you**' and Jesus Christ is 'the same yesterday and today and forever.' Hebrews 13:5,8.

3. Not only will He never drive us away but He will never stop loving us. 'The Lord's lovingkindnesses indeed **never** cease, for His compassions never fail. They are new every morning.' Lamentations 3:22,23 NASB. And nothing can separate me from that love. (Romans 8:39).

4. God is totally 'for' us and Jesus is interceding for us right now. (Romans 8:31-34). And therefore I know that 'His goodness and love will follow me all the days of my life.' Psalm 23:6.

There are many, many more spiritual certainties like these. Some will be more relevant to us than others in the different seasons of our lives. We can take God at His word, and as we thank Him for what He shows us about Himself in His Word, we can find our 'rest of faith'. We can 'rest' our lives on our unchanging God, in times of great uncertainty.

Activation . . .

It's good to have a list of certainties from God's word on which to 'rest' yourself.

Today find those 'certainties' from His word that are relevant to your life and circumstances, so that you are ready with them and able to thank God for them when the temptation to fear or worry comes upon you.

DAY 88 | Thanksgiving for God's good plans for us

Another real spiritual certainty, upon which we can rest our lives is that our God, who has paid such a great price for us on the cross to bring us into His family as His well loved sons and daughters, has great plans for us. How do we know that? Well we have probably heard that verse. "'For I know the plans I have for you," declares the Lord," plans to prosper you and not to harm you, plans to give you a hope and a future".' Jeremiah 29:11.

It may have been given to us as an encouragement, and that is what it is, but when we realise the context in which it was spoken, our faith should soar. It was in fact a promise God gave through Jeremiah to the nation of Israel in the midst of a great judgment on their apostasy. They were His people, but they had strayed badly from the Lord's ways, forgetting His love and goodness.

We on the other hand are His redeemed children, and because we live this side of the cross, any and all judgement that we have ever deserved, or will ever deserve, has fallen onto Jesus. 'But He was pierced for our transgressions, He was crushed for our iniquities; the punishment that bought us peace was upon Him', Isaiah 53:5. Not only has the cross bought us freedom from judgement, His resurrection has brought us into His family, and into a completely new life.

We are now – as one children's chorus puts it – 'Kids of the King', destined to be 'conformed to the likeness of His Son'. (Romans 8:29,30) to become like Jesus Himself. That being the case, we can be absolutely certain that His plans are indeed to prosper us and not to harm us. He has invested the very life of His Son in us. His plans, are good ones. No doubt about that at all!!

So there are three good reasons to thank Him for this wonderful truth. The first is just out of sheer gratitude, when we realise that we have a God who is on our side, and on our case. A God who loves us and is going to make us like Jesus.

The second reason for giving thanks that He has good plans for us is that it denotes our agreement with the Lord, and our embracing of His plans for us. Our thanksgiving communicates our surrender to His agenda. In thanking Him for His plans we are saying, "Your will not mine be done" as Jesus did, lest we find ourselves fighting Him over those plans and missing the goodness in them.

You see some of those plans may be good but not necessarily comfortable. God has not promised us a trouble free existence, but rather that His refining presence will be with us wherever He leads. Paul doubtless didn't deliberately sign up for prison, but he was able to write to the Philippians that, as a result of his chains, the Gospel had been preached to the whole palace guard, (Philippians 1:12,13), and so he was greatly blessed.

God's ways and thoughts are in fact higher than ours. When Jesus was questioned about John, He honoured him saying, "Among those born of women there has not risen anyone greater than John the Baptist", Matthew 11:11. John was not abandoned in prison by God, but in fact God's plan had been to take him home.

These might be dramatic examples, but I just want to distinguish 'good plans' and 'plans to prosper us' from an 'everything coming up roses' mentality. I do in fact believe that God's plans for us very often include a great deal of joy and many blessings, but our thanksgiving that His plans for us are good, need to carry us through those difficult times when we don't understand. Our thanksgiving will keep us with a heavenly perspective, remembering that the ultimate goal is to hear Him say, "Well done good and faithful servant..." Matthew 25:21.

The third and final reason for thanking Him for His good plans and purposes, is that our thanksgiving will keep us tuned into our wonderful Heavenly Father's voice, enabling us to discern in the different situations in which we find ourselves exactly what He is doing. It will keep us tracking with the Lord in joy and peace.

Activation ...

Today give thanks in your circumstances that His plans for you are good. Bless Him and enable yourself to discern His loving hand at work in your life.

DAY 89 | Thanksgiving that draws us close to God

Someone who understood that God's intent was to bless and prosper him was King David. He himself could have penned those words of Jeremiah's, "For I know the plans I have for you, "declares the Lord," plans to prosper you and not to harm you, plans to give you a hope and a future", Jeremiah 29:11. While thinking about this I was drawn again to Psalm 16, David's testimony that, through all the ups and downs of his life, he set his face to walk with God. He was able in both triumph and tragedy, to believe in the goodness of God's heart intention towards him. It's no wonder he was called 'a man after God's own heart'. Acts 13:22

This Psalm starts with David's prayer for protection and his declaration that he is making God his refuge, his safe place in life. Now we know that God had huge plans for David, but also that, in the mix, David had his enemies and his own personal failings. He certainly needed God to be his refuge.

Then further on in the psalm we have his wonderful declaration of surrender to, and trust in, God's goodness towards him. He writes 'Lord, I have chosen you alone as my inheritance. You are my prize, my pleasure and my portion. I leave my destiny and it's timing in your hands, your pleasant paths lead me to pleasant places. I'm overwhelmed by the privileges that come with following you, for you have given me the best'. Psalm 16:5,6. TPT.

David's experience of God, helps us to understand that we will experience many of the blessings that are promised to us, as we stay very close to Him in our hearts and become more aware of His closeness to us at all times. David puts it like this 'I have set the Lord always before me. Because He is at my right hand I will not be shaken. Therefore my heart is glad and my glory (my inner self) rejoices; my body too shall rest and confidently dwell in safety.' Psalm 16:8,9. AMP. Because the Lord is central to his every move David experiences joy in the Lord through his emotions, his spirit, and even his physical body,

The Passion Translation puts it this way, 'Because you are close to me and always available, my confidence will never be shaken, for I experience your wrap around presence every moment'. This is, I believe, what thanksgiving does for us. It enables us to sense His wrap around presence at all times and in all places. What David experiences seems to be similar to the 'abiding' that Jesus spoke of in John 15; that experience of closeness that brings life.

David ends the psalm (verse 11) with the lovely statement 'You have made known to me the path of life; you will fill me with joy in your presence, with eternal pleasures at your right hand.' We need to remember here that 'eternal' for us has already started, so this is not just pleasures when we get to heaven, but those wonderful surprises and interventions that happen in our lives here on earth. Those moments that come straight from the heart of God to us, in the here and now.

David knows that he has a destiny and that God will be his refuge and will guide and lead him. He knows that God's plans for him will be good, and full of joys and pleasures. He had insight into that promise from God to prosper His people and to give them a future and a hope, spoken out hundreds of years later by Jeremiah.

David knew that the best way to appropriate all the blessings of God was to keep very close to Him. Thanking God was a big part of that, and he often sang it out 'Give thanks to the Lord for He is good' Psalm 106:1. So let us like David live every day thanking God and placing Him right before us, right at the centre, then we can expect our days to be full of joy in His presence, as we experience some of those eternal pleasures that are at His right hand forevermore.

Activation ...

Thank God today that the set of His heart towards you is to bless and prosper you. He needs no persuading. It's you and me that are sometimes slow to believe!

DAY 90 | 'Thank you' – The password of faith!

We live in an age of passwords, user names and ID access codes. I find it quite a strain to remember them all and no doubt, although we are asked not to, most of us have them all written down somewhere, perhaps in a notebook under the bed!!

Throughout the last three months on our journey of thanksgiving, I hope that like me you have discovered that 'Thank you' is a key password that enables us to reach our Heavenly Father's ear. As we have focused on giving thanks to Him in so many different situations and scenarios, we have in fact been expressing our faith in Him, and in His rich supply of grace to us.

Paul wrote, 'God is able to make all grace abound toward you so that in all things at all times, having all that you need, you will abound to every good work.' 2 Corinthians 9:8. Those words come after his previous encouragement that they should give freely and cheerfully. Generally we look at those verses as being a promise that God will honour our financial giving by giving back to us, in a material way, all that we need for His service; but what if it's more than that?

In an earlier meditation we saw that Paul encouraged the Christian at Thessalonica to 'give thanks in all circumstances, for this is God's will for you in Christ Jesus.' 1 Thessalonians 5:18. This can sometimes feel like a heavy duty thing, especially if the circumstances really don't seem good and we don't 'feel' like giving thanks to anyone for anything.

But what if we now begin to see that 'giving thanks' is actually our password not just through the gates into God's presence, Psalm 100:4, but into His abundant supply of whatever we are needing for that time and circumstance.

If, instead of thanking God through gritted teeth, because that what is 'required' of us, we 'offer' our thanks joyfully and freely as an expression of faith in His love for us, and goodness that He will 'meet all our need according to His glorious riches in Christ Jesus', Philippians 4:19, then our faith will indeed be released, and we will find ourselves drawing on that abundant supply of 'grace sufficient' as it flows towards us.

I know it sounds circular and in a sense it is. Once I see what is freely mine 'in Christ' of God's grace and favour, then any and every situation becomes a wonderful opportunity to receive more from Him. I will then be more than ready to offer up my thanksgiving in anticipation for what I am going to receive from Him. Thanksgiving releases faith that then unlocks to me the vast resources of heaven that are already now mine in Christ.

Activation . . .

Remember that it was Jesus who said, 'I came that they may have life, and have it abundantly.' John 10:10. RSV. May be it's time to have a look at those aspects of life where you know that you need more from the Lord, and intentionally thank Him that He is with you in these areas with His grace and abundant provision. As you give thanks, claim that promise that He can and will make all grace abound towards you in all things, so that you yourself can abound in every good work. (2 Corinthians 9:8)

DAY 91 | Thanksgiving and JOY

I was thinking today about 'Joy'. It's such an important emotion for, apart from making us feel good, it gives us strength and energy. The oft quoted words, "The joy of the Lord is your strength", Nehemiah 8:10, are now validated by neurological science, but joy is also something spiritual, and God in His love chose to create us as spiritual beings with the capacity to feel this thing we call 'joy'.

Joy, like real love, has its source in God. It is one of His attributes, an integral part of His personality. Heaven is full of joy, and joy is at the heart of the Trinity. When Jesus came to earth as a baby to fulfill God's great plan of salvation, the shepherds were told by the angels, 'Do not be afraid for I bring you good tidings of great joy.' Luke 2:10. All of heaven was so excited by what was about to happen, and they were expecting the news to bring 'great joy' to earth too.

And so it continued, Jesus was able to tell the people 'there is joy in the presence of the angels over one sinner who repents' Luke 15:10. He was able to endure the cross in anticipation of the 'great joy' before Him as many people would become Christians and join His ever growing Kingdom. Hebrews 12:2. Even in the Old Testament we read that the Lord has great joy over His people when they turn to Him and let Him help them. Zephaniah 3:17.

It would seem that much of God's joy is found in loving and saving us, in bringing us into relationship with Himself. Amazing as it may seem, we are actually a source of joy to Him. It is no wonder then, that as His children, we find our 'fullness of joy' 'in His presence.' Psalm 16:11.

We can even experience joy in difficult circumstances, as we walk in the knowledge that He is with us. If we look at Psalm 23, for example, we can see that David experiences more than a hint of joy, as he sees the Lord spreading a table before him in the presence of his enemies. He writes 'You anoint my head with oil, my cup overflows'. Now that is a testimony of joy in a time of trouble.

If we give Jesus and the Father joy, what about the Holy Spirit. Well I think the Holy Spirit is the person of the Godhead who imparts the joy of heaven into our spirits. The Kingdom of heaven, we are told is not a matter of eating and drinking, but of 'righteousness, joy and peace in the Holy Spirit', Romans 14:17. Joy, one of the fruit of the Spirit, Galatians 5:22, is definitely one of the real benefits of staying full of the Spirit.

We are made in God's image, and are capable of receiving His joy within ourselves and giving Him joy in return. Now that is what I call an exciting and wonderful relationship! There is joy in His presence as we get close to Him, and joy in the Holy Spirit as He fills us. There is joy in our connection to Father, Son and Holy Spirit.

Over these past three months as we have meditated on the power of thanksgiving to transform our lives, we can look back and see that 'giving thanks' helps us to war against the things that rob us of our joy. Things like doubt, unbelief, unforgiveness, criticism and fear that can fill our minds, and seep into our spirits. These negatives are the antithesis of joy, and the devil can robs us (John 10:10), by getting us to toy with, and ruminate on them, thereby stifling the things that the Holy Spirit wants to fill us with, like joy.

Activation . . .

Today, as you dwell on the truth that we have a joy filled God who wants to fill us with His joy, thank Him that He made you with the capacity to experience joy.

Thank Him that through these daily meditations He has and is taking you on a wonderful journey to discover the power that thanksgiving can have in your life.

In Proverbs 4:23 we are advised 'Above all else, guard your heart, for it is the wellspring of life.' Thank Him that in thanksgiving He has given you a weapon with which you can guard your heart from the negatives that your enemy wants to plant your heart.

I believe the Lord is ready to release a blessing of joy over you, whatever your current circumstances. Your thanksgiving will draw you close to Him and you will find His joy filling you again and again.

What next?

This book is the first of four taking you through 365 days of meditations on the power of thanksgiving to transform your life. We plan to publish book two in this series of four in the spring of 2023.

We pray that, as you have read and pondered these daily devotionals, you have absorbed some more of the relentless love that God has for you, and that you have been drawn closer to Him day by day.

For some, the four books may take you through a year, others may find it more helpful to travel through the books more slowly, taking longer.

I believe there will be lasting benefit in reading through all four books in a regular rhythm, at the pace that suits you best; we are all different.

If you would like to purchase further copies of this book or order the next in the series, Book 2, then please email us at:

enquiries@lifetraining.co.uk.